MILT TANZER

HOW TO
BUY OR SELL
YOUR HOME
WITHOUT
A BROKER

Prentice
Hall Press

A member of Penguin Putnam Inc.
375 Hudson Street, New York, N.Y. 10014
www.penguinputnam.com

CIP Data is available from the Library of Congress

Printed in the United States of America

10   9   8   7   6   5   4   3   2

ISBN 0-7352-0289-3

CONTENTS

PART THREE
WORKING WITH APPRAISERS, INSPECTORS, AND OTHER PROFESSIONALS

INTRODUCTION

Most home buyers and sellers feel that they must employ a real estate broker to buy or sell their home—and that is just what real estate brokers want you to think. Attorneys want you to believe you cannot prepare a will without an attorney—and that's what they want you to believe. CPAs want you to think you cannot prepare your income taxes, and gain the maximum tax savings advantages, without a CPA—and that's what they want you to believe.

This brings up an interesting question. Why would a real estate broker write a book on how to buy or sell your home without a broker? No, I'm not trying to put real estate brokers out of business. The truth is that many would-be home sellers or buyers would like to do it themselves in order to save paying a real estate commission. It does not matter what we, as real estate professionals say, those sellers or buyers will still do it themselves. Unfortunately, many of them could, and often do, make a huge financial mistake or get totally frustrated with all that is involved in marketing or buying a home. You purchased this book because you want to be able to do it yourself. *How to Buy or Sell Your Home Without a Broker* will guide you through the process and help you avoid the financial mistakes and frustrations that many do-it-yourselfers often face.

This book is filled with the methods and techniques used by professional real estate brokers to successfully market your home or find the best deal on the purchase of a home. Above all, it shows you, step by step, how to avoid the pitfalls most homebuyers and sellers experience. The information here has been compiled from my 30 years' experience as a broker, working with countless other professionals as well as home buyers and sellers.

Unfortunately, selling your home requires more than putting a sign on the property and waiting for the offers to come in. Likewise, finding the best home for your needs and budget requires more than knocking on the door of a For Sale By Owner (FSBO, pronounced "fizzbo") and handing them a purchase contract.

This is a "how to" book that will explain everything you need to know. You will be led through each process, step by step, from beginning to end. You will learn how to avoid making a costly mistake, whether you are a buyer or a seller. You will also learn the trade secrets of real estate brokers who want you to believe you need them to buy or sell a home successfully.

Unlike most of the other books on the market, this is the only one you will need as a buyer or a seller. It has been divided into three parts: Part One is a home seller guide. Part Two is a home buyer guide. Part Three explains how to work with various professionals you may need and what they do. A glossary is also included.

Because it contains all of this information, you will be able to learn from everyone who is involved in buying or selling a home—buyers, sellers, brokers, appraisers, home inspectors, etc.

This knowledge will aid you in planning your own home-marketing or home-buying tactics. The CD-ROM program that accompanies this book includes an interactive tutorial based on the book plus forms and checklists you can print to use when house hunting or preparing your home for sale. It also includes calculators to figure mortgage payments, the benefits of a shorter-term mortgage, and both buyer and seller closing statements ready to fill in the blanks.

By the time you finish this book, you will know more about buying or selling a home than many real estate brokers. Most important, you will know how to avoid the traps and mistakes most "do it yourselfers" experience. You'll also avoid the other big problem buyers and sellers frequently face when doing it on their own—discouragement. It takes work and knowledge to do it right and get results. Many buyers or sellers list with a broker because they do not know what they are doing and become discouraged. You are about to change all of that with this book. In the process, you will save thousands of dollars in real estate commissions.

Milt Tanzer

PART ONE

SELLING
YOUR HOME
YOURSELF

There is more to selling a home than just making the decision to sell, putting an ad in the paper, or a sign in the front yard, and waiting for someone to knock on your door with a contract to purchase at a price you like.

We begin with the decision to sell your home. Should you sell or just renovate your present home and stay where you are? You'll learn the pros and cons of each alternative.

Once you decide to sell, you will learn what you need to know to sell it successfully without a broker. We'll include many of the methods brokers use to insure a successful sale as well as a checklist of tips on selling a home.

Now for the part that many sellers overlook: preparing your home for sale. You'll be led, step-by-step, through what you MUST do to be successful in selling and why you need to do it. You'll learn the correct way to hold an open house, and just as important, how to protect yourself and your belongings when you do it. You'll find out what must be done to make the home show well.

We'll discuss the other factors involved in selling your home, such as Comparative Market Analyses (CMAs) and how vitally important they are to your success. You'll even learn how to prepare for home inspections and why they will be almost a certainty when you sell. Pricing your home is vital to making it competitive and still profitable. You'll find out how to do it.

Another consideration is: What do you do if your home doesn't sell? What do you do now? What do you do if you're in financial trouble and cannot make mortgage payments? Learn ways of solving these problems.

Next, you'll attend a closing. You'll learn how to estimate your closing cost and proceeds from the sale, what you need to take to the closing, what can possibly go wrong, and what you can do about it.

CHAPTER 1

MAKING THE DECISION TO SELL

The average family will sell its present home once every seven years. If you buy your first home at age twenty-five and follow the normal trend until you are age sixty-five, you will move about six times.

REASONS FOR SELLING

What is the reason for moving so often? There are several:

1. *Your family is growing:* As your family increases in size you need additional living space, more bedrooms, etc.

2. *Your family is shrinking:* Your children grow up and leave home so you need less space. These people are often referred to as "empty nesters."

3. *Your job requires you to move:* Moving to a different location due to employment transfers or job changes.

4. *You've had changes in your financial status:* Your financial situation changes so you need to adjust your living accommodations accordingly. You may want a more expensive home or a less expensive home.

5. *You've had a life change:* This often prompts a change in living status. You may want to move nearer your children or just downsize your living accommodations.

CONSIDERING RENOVATION

We've mentioned the various reasons for moving. Now let's examine each of them from the point of view of renovating your present home rather than selling.

CHANGE IN SPACE REQUIREMENTS

Perhaps your family has grown and moved out so a home that once accommodated four or five people now serves for two. The first impulse you may have is, "Why do we need all of this space? We can move into a much smaller home and save some money."

Carefully compare the alternative of moving to that of staying where you are. Will you be happy in a new location and in a smaller home? Figure out how much money you will really save including mortgage payments, insurance, taxes, utility bills, etc. Quite often the difference in cost may not be large enough to make it worthwhile. Here is how to determine it. On a piece of paper make two columns, one with the heading "Present Home" and the second labeled "New Home." First, in the left margin, write down "Market Value" (of the house you now own and the one you may consider buying). Under that, enter the amount of the mortgage, followed by the equity you will have in each (market value minus mortgage amount). Then estimate your closing cost to sell one home and buy another. (We'll cover how to determine these costs later. For now, we'll just use the estimated figures we filled in below.) Next, list the expense factors in the left margin: Mortgage Principal and Interest Payments, Real Estate Taxes, Homeowner Insurance, Estimated Utility Bills (water, sewer, electric, heating, etc.). Use monthly figures for your analysis.

Now add all these expense amounts together and compare your present monthly cash outlay with the proposed expenses in "New Home" column. It might look like this:

	PRESENT HOME	**NEW HOME**
Market Value	$175,000	$125,000
Mortgage	75,000	50,000
Closing Costs	5,000	4,000
Mortgage Payments/Mo.	$ 717	$ 388
Real Estate Taxes	300	250
Homeowner Insurance	100	75
Utilities	250	175
Total Monthly Expenses	$ 1,367	$ 888

In our example, your monthly operating expenses will be reduced by $479 a month. Now you need to decide, first, how important that savings is to your budget, and second, how happy you will be in your new, smaller home. In any case, it is a simple matter to estimate the cost of your two alternatives. One more point to consider. You will be facing closing costs on both the home you are selling and the home you are buying. In our example, it amounts to about $9,000. That is a $9,000 reduction in your equity. It will take you a year and a half of cost savings on your new home to recoup that loss.

YOUR FAMILY HAS GROWN

This is the opposite problem. Now you are facing a situation where you only have a two-bedroom home and two children who refuse to sleep in the same room together. Your first impulse will be to sell and get a larger home. The other alternative you have, short of waiting for one of the children to grow up and get married, is to add on to your existing home. If zoning allows and you like your present home, this may be an excellent alternative. Not only will it cost less than moving to a new, larger home but you eliminate the hassle of packing, moving, changing addresses, possibly phone numbers, utility registration, voter registration, perhaps school districts, etc. You also avoid losing your neighbors, assuming you get along with them. If, on the other hand, your next-door neighbor insists on letting his Doberman use your yard as a bathroom, that may be enough motivation to make you want to move. Unfortunately, you could discover that your next-door neighbor at your new home has a Great Dane.

CHANGE IN FINANCIAL STATUS

This reason for moving is self-explanatory. Your financial status has changed one of two ways, up or down. If it has gone up, you may want to move into a larger, more expensive home in a better neighborhood; if the opposite, you may find it necessary to move into a less expensive home. The motivating factor here is not a space need but a financial need (or desire). This decision to move will be made on that basis. Renovating your present home will, obviously, not solve this problem.

RETIREMENT NEEDS

If you are retired, you may want the freedom to come and go as you please without having to worry about your home. This is the period in life when senior citizens move into maintained communities and condominiums. Not only are they worry-free, but most offer full-time security. You are able to lock your door and leave for as long as you wish without worrying about your home.

THE NEED FOR RENOVATION

After you have lived in your home for several years, it begins to look shabby...unless you have been careful to maintain it, which you should be doing. We're not talking about paint and landscaping here which most homeowners provide for. What does require consideration is an outdated kitchen with fifteen-year-old appliances, a ten-year-old heating and air conditioning system, old and worn bathroom fixtures, carpet and tile badly worn, etc. There are also such things as the roof. Roofs only last so long and then need replacing.

This is when some homeowners decide it's time to sell. They believe that selling their present home and moving is a better solution than upgrading. In most cases, they are wrong. Why? Because no one else will want to buy it in its present condition. If someone does, you can be sure the price will be negotiated down to cover upgrading the kitchen and appliances, new bathrooms, carpeting and tile and may even include the cost of knocking out a wall or two to give the home the modern-day "open" look. And expect the building inspector to find every flaw possible. The inspection will also check out the roof, signs of termites and dry rot, and the air conditioning and heating system.

The bottom line is simple. If you'd rather sell your home than remodel and upgrade it, you can expect to sell it for a lot less than what it may be worth in an improved condition. A few years ago, I listed a home in a nice neighborhood. It was badly in need of painting. I suggested that, in that condition, the home was worth $125,000 because it showed very badly. I told the owner that the fair market value of similar homes sold was closer to $135,000. To back up my comments, all of the associates toured his house during one of our weekly sales meeting inspections of new listings. Each one, independently, confirmed my belief that the fair market value of the home was in the $125,000 range, if he was lucky and found someone who really liked the location and floor plan. Reluctantly, he spent $3,000 painting the house. It sold within two weeks for $135,000. Needless to say he was very pleased with my recommendation.

The point is simple. If you have a home that needs $25,000 worth of upgrading, and that is your motivation to sell, you can expect to make at least $25,000 less on the sale. If, however, the home is in a deteriorating neighborhood, you may want to sell before values drop any further. A home in need of renovation in an otherwise good neighborhood will have to be renovated. You either do it yourself, stay there and enjoy your newly updated home or sell it in its present condition and take the loss. Only you can decide the better alternative for you.

TIMING YOUR SALE

The first thing we need to discuss is timing. When should you sell your home? There are several factors you need to consider.

IS IT A BUYER'S MARKET OR A SELLER'S MARKET?

You are in a buyer's market when there is an abundance of homes available for sale. This gives the buyer a larger choice of homes from which to choose. It also gives the buyer more negotiating power. "I can buy the same house in the next block for $15,000 less than you are asking," or, "The Smith home a couple blocks from here has a new roof and the kitchen has been updated. With the exception of that, both homes are comparable. My offer is based on what I feel your home is worth, compared with your competition." In a buyer's market a seller who is serious about selling will negotiate on the price and terms.

A seller who has had a home on the market for a few months is an even better candidate for negotiating on a price. Such a seller will realize that selling a home is not an automatic transaction where buyers are lined up with a contract in hand, ready to outbid each other. A wise seller must also recognize that the longer a home stays on the market, the less its chances to sell. Unless a buyer has just entered the home buying market, he or she will know if a home has been on the market for a long time and "just hasn't sold." The automatic assumption will be that there is either something wrong with the house or it is so overpriced no one wants it. In either case, a potential buyer will pass on it and go to a fresher listing.

If you want to sell your home, and find yourself in a buyer's market, you can do one of two things:

1. Hold off marketing your home until the market shifts to your favor (a seller's market).

2. Price your home aggressively enough to attract a buyer quickly.

The first few weeks that your home is on the market is when you will attract the most attention. A "just listed" ad in the paper or a new

"For Sale" sign in the front yard will attract attention for the first week or two. After that, your activity will diminish . . . and the longer your home is on the market, the less activity you will realize. Finally, no one will consider it worth looking at, even someone who is just entering the market. Someone is sure to tell a new buyer, "You can forget about the home on Elm Street. It's been on the market for months. There must be something wrong with it."

Don't fall into that trap, unless you really don't care if you sell. And you shouldn't put your home on the market until you are motivated to sell.

The home sale market is always changing. If you can afford to wait until you are in a seller's market, do it. Then there are many buyers looking for a home, but very few homes available for sale. Now the seller is in command, and can often demand, and get top price for a property. Now is the time to sell.

> **CAUTION:** Don't use a seller's market as a chance to "make a killing" on the sale of your home. If your home is worth only $150,000, don't expect someone to rush in and pay you $200,000, even if homes are difficult to find. There is always something on the market that will be priced close to fair market value that will overshadow your overpriced listing. You may get lucky and find someone who does not know the market but falls in love with your home and will pay more than it is worth, but that is rare. Generally your home will not sell and suddenly you will be back in a buyer's market. Not only will you have lost your chance to sell, but also putting the home back on the market at a later date will lessen the impact you want as a fresh listing on the market. You just read what can happen if your home already has a reputation for being a "dog" on the market; it will be tainted.

A Point to Remember: Under most circumstances, the best time to sell your home is in the first three or four weeks it comes on the market. That's when you will receive the most interest and the most activity. The longer it remains on the market after that initial period, the less the chance you have of selling.

In the chapter on pricing your home, we will discuss a problem common to many sellers. They price their home, not on what it is worth on today's market, but on how much money they need to get out of it to buy a larger home or to support themselves financially. I've had many buyers who have done just that. When asked how much they thought their home was worth, they have said, "$200,000." When I have asked them how they arrived at that figure, after showing them that comparable homes in the area were selling for about $150,000, the answer usually was, "Well, we owe about $75,000 on it, which will leave us with $125,000 when we sell. That's how much we need to live on for the next few years."

That approach to establishing a selling price may sound far fetched, but you'd be surprised how many sellers think that way. I hope you are not one of them!

One final comment about buyer's vs. seller's market. There seems to be an unwritten law that states, "When you decide to sell your home, you will always discover that you are in a buyer's market. When you want to buy, you will always be in a seller's market." I think a fellow named Murphy might have discovered that law a long time ago.

If your need to buy or sell is not an urgent one, *always* wait until the home market is in your favor.

'TIS THE SEASON!

We've already discussed buyer's market vs. seller's market. Another factor affects the timing of selling your home—the season or time of the year.

Depending on the area in which you live, you know that there are certain times of the year when the most potential homebuyers are looking. There are two main factors for this seasonal market.

1. Winter vs. Summer: If you live in the north, there will be far fewer buyers looking for a home when there is snow and ice on the ground than in the warm spring, summer or fall months. Conversely, if you live in the "tropical" area of the country, the seasons are not that important. In fact, the best market for selling a home in Florida is

during the winter months, when the "snow birds" have migrated out of the frozen north to the sunny, warm climate of tropical Florida.

2. Schools enter into the picture. Most homebuyers with school age children will not be in the house market during the months when school is in session. Most will, if they can, wait until the school year is almost over before beginning their search for a new home. Ideally, they want to move after their children are out of school, especially if they must relocate to another school district or, even worse, out of the area altogether. Switching children from one school to another during the school year is difficult for the children as well as for the parents. Adjusting to a new school at the beginning of a new school year is hard for a child, but not so confusing as doing it in the middle of the school year.

OTHER FACTORS

There are two other circumstances that precipitate a time to sell.

1. Transfer by a company to a new location often causes a homeowner to move with disregard for either the season or school situation.

2. Another reason is not, unfortunately, a pleasant one but rather one of necessity. The homeowner may be forced to move for several reasons:

   a. Loss of a job. The breadwinner must relocate to find employment.

   b. Loss of a spouse. Many husbands or wives feel compelled to move soon after losing a spouse. Although the experts advise not to make any quick decision along these lines, there may be motivating circumstances that require it. These include an inability to afford to remain in the home, the need for a support group such as children who live in another town or state, or just the haunting memories of the past. Whatever the reason, listen to the advice of the experts in that area, if you are ever faced with this situation. Don't make any sudden, rash changes in your lifestyle that will make life even more complicated than it has already become.

c. You can no longer afford the cost of your present home. (If this is your situation, be sure to read the section entitled, "What to do if you are in financial trouble.")

d. Upsizing: You need a larger home, either because you have a growing family or you can now afford a larger, better home.

e. Downsizing: The first reason you may want to downsize is that your children are grown and no longer live with you. You no longer need the room or the expense of a larger home.

The second reason to downsize is because you have reached retirement age and you want to be free to come and go as you please and not have to worry about caring for a large home. A condominium may be your answer, where you can just lock the doors and leave whenever you wish.

Unless circumstances dictate otherwise, always select the time of the year when the most homebuyers are out looking so that you can obtain the top market value. Always take time to think through your decision to sell. Your home is probably your most valuable possession. Don't make any financial mistakes.

CHAPTER 2

SELLING YOUR HOME SUCCESSFULLY

There are several things you need to be aware of before we begin talking about selling your home yourself. As soon as you put an ad in the newspaper or a sign in your front yard that proclaims, "I'm selling my house myself," you can expect your phone to ring off the hook. Don't get excited. It will no doubt be every real estate broker in town who saw your ad or sign, looking for a listing.

If you are a typical home seller, you will be faced with the "chicken or the egg" dilemma. Here is how it affects you. You probably cannot afford to own two houses at once. This means you must wait for the proceeds from the sale of your present home before you can buy another one. If you sell your home before you purchase another one, you may have no place to live when your present house closes until you buy another. So what comes first—sell your home or try to buy another before your home is sold? When we discuss financing, you'll see how you can have the better of two worlds, and not have to live on the street for a month or two.

KNOW THE MARKET

Before you consider putting your home on the market for sale, you need to know how much it is worth, or better yet, how much you can get for it. This is probably the most critical step in selling your home and the one that many home sellers fail to research and take seriously. Most sellers will decide how much cash they need out of the home and price it accordingly, regardless of how much it is really worth. Sellers often price their home based on the "Mine is better than the Smiths' house" theory. The Smiths have their home on the market for $175,000. There are all kinds of reasons yours is worth a lot more. It was freshly painted three years ago while the Smiths' home hasn't been painted for five years. You also removed a wall to open up the living and dining rooms. You love it that way and you know your home increased in value $10,000 because of it. What you don't take into consideration is, you may love it but a potential buyer may have preferred it the way it was. You have six ceiling fans throughout your home and the Smiths have none. The list goes on and on but the bottom line is simple. You feel that if the Smiths' house is on the market for $175,000, then yours must be worth at least $225,000. (Your home usually ends up overpriced and does not sell. More on this subject in Chapter 7.)

An even worse mistake is to underprice your home. You could lose thousands of dollars because you did not take the time or did not know how to determine fair market value of your home.

You need to determine the real value of your home so you do not make either of the mistakes we just discussed. You need to check out existing homes on the market, gather complete information on each and compare them with yours. But keep in mind: Those sellers could also have overstated the listed price. Most sellers price a home with the expectation of having to negotiate the price to close the deal. "The house may have a fair market value of $175,000 but let's put it on the market at $195,000 in order to give us some negotiating room." When a real estate broker handles a sale, the seller will want to price it even higher to cover the broker's fee.

DETERMINING FAIR MARKET VALUE

Fair Market Value is the selling price of a home based on what the seller is willing to accept and the buyer is willing to pay. It is established the same way as any other product that is for sale, by supply and demand. When we are in a seller's market (more buyers than there are homes for sale), home prices will increase. When we are in a buyer's market (more homes for sale than there are buyers for them), home prices will decrease. (This of course is tempered by mortgage interest rates and the general condition of the economy.)

This brings us to the question: "How do I determine the value of my home, assuming I really want to sell it?" There are a couple of ways. We briefly mentioned checking other, comparable homes for sale in your area. This is, as you now know, the least accurate way of determining market value because it relies on other sellers who may be trying to make a killing on their home sale.

You can go to the courthouse property records department and research the past sales on properties you know have sold in the last year in your neighborhood. This information is a matter of public record and available to anyone. Someone in the County Clerk's office will show you how. I'll warn you up front, however: It can be a time-consuming process, depending on how updated the county's record system is, computer wise.

USING COMPARATIVE MARKET ANALYSIS (CMA)

The best and easiest way to determine the value of your home is to have a Comparative Market Analysis (CMA) prepared. A CMA will show you what homes are currently on the market and at what asking price, what homes have sold in the past year (or whatever time frame you wish) and what they sold for. It is the accurate method used by brokers to determine the market value of a home. How do you obtain a CMA on your property? There is a good chance your County has a web site with the same information on it that you can get by researching property sales at the courthouse. You may be able to pinpoint your neighborhood for the search. Again, it's a matter of public record and available to anyone.

HOW A CMA IS GENERATED

A CMA is arrived at by using four different factors:

1. Currently Listed Properties: What is on the market that is comparable to your home and what the asking price is of these homes.

    Important Point: When discussing CMAs the term "comparable" is used. The only way a CMA will be of value to you in establishing a fair market value is if all of the homes being compared have the same basic features as yours. This means size, number of bedrooms and baths, special amenities, lot size, condition, immediate neighborhood, etc. If any of these factors vary widely from your home, the selling prices need to be adjusted up or down to compensate for the differences.

2. Recently Sold Properties: Number one above compares your home to others that are currently for sale. We all know that the listed price of a home may vary greatly from the price at which it will finally sell. That makes the Recently Sold Properties a much better indication of property values. Generally, because home prices tend to go up, you want the comparable sales to be within the past twelve months. A home that sold five years ago, even though it is identical to yours in every way, may not be a reliable indicator of the current value of your home.

    If the Currently Listed Property method isn't much good in determining real value, why use it? The main reason is to show you what you are competing against in your market. By seeing other homes that are for sale, you can judge how yours compares. The second reason is that there may not be many or any comparable sales from which to estimate value.

3. Pending Sales: These are homes that are currently under contract but have not yet closed. Generally all you have to go on, until the deal is closed, is the original asking price. It is rare when you can find out how much it sold for until it closes and becomes a matter of public record.

4. Properties That Fail to Sell: The final component of fair market value is an analysis of comparable properties that failed to sell. Here you have a chance to examine the homes on that list and compare them with yours. You can usually see why the home did not sell. Most often, the seller was not motivated to sell and the home was priced well above fair market value.

Appraisers will use all four of these comparisons in determining the fair market value of a property. They will make adjustments in the comparables they found in order to give a fair estimate of market value. They will add value to your home if it is newer than the comparable. They will adjust the value based on amenities, square footage, location, etc. After all of the information is collected, and adjustments made, an estimate of fair market value for your home is determined. The report you receive will list all of the various comparables so you can see how the value of your home was established.

One final caution about overpricing. When your home first goes on the market, you can expect a lot of activity, both from real estate brokers and from potential buyers. (By the way, several of your neighbors will want to know how much you want for your home. That way they will think, "Oh, my house is much nicer than theirs, so I know it's worth more.") Keep in mind that newly listed properties gain the most attention, traffic and potential buyers. Potential buyers who look at your home and realize it is overpriced, compared with others they have seen, will just walk away and you will never see them again. As time goes on, you will see less and less activity. The word spreads quickly, especially in the real estate broker community, that your home is overpriced so don't waste your time on it. Remember that thought if you decide to list your home with a broker who will take it at any price just to get the listing. Eventually you'll have to lower your price to a more realistic level. Unfortunately, everyone already knew about it when it was overpriced. Chances are they will not be tempted to come back after the price is lowered.

The solution is simple. If you are not motivated to sell at close to fair market value, do not put your home on the market!

HOW MUCH DO YOU KNOW ABOUT YOUR HOME?

As a home seller, you will be asked questions about the physical condition of the property. Although your buyer will have a home inspection done (discussed in Chapter 17), there are certain things a home inspector will not find. Some of these defects, flaws or area changes are important to disclose to a potential buyer, if they are known to you. Let me give you a couple of examples:

EXAMPLE NUMBER 1

You know that there are some structural problems with your home. In order to patch them up, you had a contractor fill in the settlement cracks and refinish the surface of the structure. You were further informed that there is a major problem here and it will continue to "sink." You'd better disclose that fact to potential buyers or you may be subject to a lawsuit.

EXAMPLE NUMBER 2

The city is talking about using the vacant land it owns behind your house for a city playground. Again, if the rumors are true, you need to disclose this fact to potential buyers. You may be able to lessen the impact by saying, "You'll never have neighbors in a high-rise apartment building backed up to your home. It will be a city park forever." Or, "It may be a playground, but the city stated it will be closed by 9:00 P.M. every night, unless there is a special event planned."

In any case, you can save yourself a lot of headaches and possible lawsuits by disclosing facts that may adversely affect your property and that are not readily visible or a matter of public record.

CHAPTER 3

PREPARING YOUR HOME FOR SALE

You need to prepare your home for sale before you ever consider putting up a "For Sale" sign. Here are some vital things to consider in the process.

First impressions count. Whenever you meet someone for the first time, you form a "first impression." Sometimes it may be misleading, but that does not matter. In your mind, you already know you do not like that person. The same holds true with your home. The minute a potential buyer pulls up in front, he or she forms a first impression of the property. Unless that impression is a good one, the buyer will probably drive off and will be gone for good. If the outside of the home is in need of sprucing up and looks cluttered, everyone will assume the inside is also in poor repair and cluttered. You don't ever want this to happen.

GENERAL GUIDELINES

Here are some general guidelines about what to look for and what needs to be done.

MAKE SURE EVERYTHING WORKS

What is the general condition of the home? How well does it show? Check such items as paint condition and dripping water faucets; make sure windows are clean; make minor repairs as needed. Pretend you are a potential buyer, or better yet a home inspector. Check out everything that is supposed to work and make sure it does. Look at the overall appearance of everything else. What can be done to improve it?

MAKE IT CLEAN

Have carpets and draperies cleaned. Make sure your kitchen and bathrooms are spotlessly clean. These are the two areas most housewives check first because they are the rooms in the home that usually become dirty more quickly. While you are in the kitchen, make sure the oven is clean. You'd be surprised how many people will check the inside of an oven for cleanliness. If the oven is clean, a potential buyer figures other "hidden" areas will also be clean. Always check under the kitchen sink; it is another area that becomes cluttered and dirty quickly because it is often overlooked. Make sure it is clean and orderly; throw out unnecessary bottles and cans of cleaning material. You can believe a potential buyer will look there.

Carry your cleaning one step further by having a pleasant aroma in the house. A fresh-smelling house will create a good impression on visitors. *Caution:* Do not overdo air fresheners. A better alternative is to have a potpourri warming on the kitchen stove. A little vanilla simmering in a pot on the stove also gives off the "homey" scent of home cooking.

Finally, watch out for pet odors. Carpet cleaning will help some, but your dog needs to be bathed to insure it does not contribute to the problem. Cats are another problem. If possible, put litter boxes outside during showings.

DO AWAY WITH CLUTTER

We all accumulate things we don't need. Unfortunately, clutter does not have a place in a home you are trying to sell. Make sure counters are clear. Check hallways and stairs for objects that need to be put away. If your home looks like a furniture warehouse, so filled with furniture that you have paths from room to room, find a way to get rid of or store some of the extra items, at least while showing your home. People love to look in closets. Unfortunately, this is where we all store too much stuff. Try to get them organized and looking less cluttered. Finally, make sure all valuables and jewelry are put away for safekeeping. (We'll remind you of this several times just to make sure you realize how important it is.)

CHECK OUT THE EXTERIOR

Is the lawn well trimmed and well kept? If some patching of bare spots is needed, do it. Touch up the exterior of the building, if it can be done without looking like a patch job. Have your shrubs neatly trimmed. Repair anything that is in need of repair. Make sure the driveway is clean and free of clutter. If it is a blacktop finish, does it need a coat of sealer to make it look fresh again?

MAKE YOUR HOME INVITING

Soft music playing in the background creates a good impression. Have all of the lights turned on, even in the daytime. Open the draperies during the day, unless the view is undesirable. You want your house to give a "Gee, I'd like to live here" impression.

INVITE THE NEIGHBORS

Ask your friends or your neighbors to give their honest opinion of how your home shows. Find out what first attracts them when looking around. Also find out what distracts them and try to improve it. You probably won't have to invite them; they will be knocking on your door as soon as they see your "For Sale" sign in the front yard. So as long as they want to check out your home and compare it (and your asking price) with their homes, ask them for their opinions and try to convince them you want an honest response, not just what they think you want to hear.

The name of the game is to make a favorable first impression on the potential buyers. If they become distracted or disturbed by something unfavorable they see, you have lost them for good.

MARKETING YOUR HOME

Once your home is ready to show, you'll want to consider holding an Open House. Now is the time to begin your advertising program. You have several choices. We'll look at each of them.

First, and foremost, put a "For Sale" sign in the front yard. As we mentioned earlier, as soon as you do this you can expect a lot of calls, mostly from real estate brokers and nosy neighbors. Don't completely disregard them. You may be able to work with a broker who claims to have a potential buyer for your home (and most of them will tell you that). Offer to let the broker show the property to a "ready buyer" and state that the price is $175,000 NET TO YOU. The broker's fee must be added on top of that net price. This will discourage many brokers because they are now competing with your lower price and keeping control of a buyer is very difficult. You also do not want to discourage neighbors. One of them may have a friend whom they would like to have as a neighbor. Of course, many will just be curious, as we discussed earlier.

NEWSPAPER ADVERTISING

There are several considerations here. If your city is large enough to have more than one major newspaper, you must decide on how to spend your advertising dollars. Should you pick just one or spread your ad out over two or more? Again, cost of advertising is not cheap and the larger the circulation a paper enjoys, the higher the per-line advertising charge will be. Also check into local neighborhood newspapers. Their circulation is small compared with that of the majors, but this means their advertising charges are also small. As a practical matter, small newspapers often draw more traffic to a home listing than the big ones will. They concentrate on the area you are in rather than the entire county or multiple county areas. You can afford to try several different ads to see which one draws the most response.

Rules for Newspaper Ads

RULE NO. 1. Do not skimp on the ad in order to save a few dollars. Your ad must entice potential buyers. Instead of saying "3/2 house in good condition," paint a verbal picture of the home. "You must see this beautiful, newly decorated 3/2 home at the end of a quiet street. Only the birds can be heard at night." What did you first notice about your home that made you fall in love with it? You have the benefit of knowing what it has to offer to potential buyers. Let them in on your secret. One more thing: Use the word "home," not "house." I think you can feel the difference.

Rule No. 2. Publish the price in your ad. If you don't, you will be flooded with phone calls from people who cannot afford your home.

Rule No. 3. Do not give the address. You can say it is located in Fairfield Lakes or a specific subdivision, but don't include the address. Why? If you publish the asking price (which you should do) and the address, you will eliminate the majority of potential buyers before you ever see them. They will drive by your home, look at the outside and think to themselves, "It sure isn't worth $175,000" and drive off. You will never get the chance to show them how nice a home it is.

Rule No. 4. Make sure your headline grabs the reader. With hundreds of ads in most newspapers, all offering homes for sale, you want yours to be noticed. One of the best headlines you can use is "FOR SALE BY OWNER." Believe me, it will make your phone ring.

Rule No. 5. Continually change your ad. Why? Home hunters will look at the paper week after week. They will begin to recognize the same ad appearing repeatedly and just pass over it. Varying the ad will also give you a chance to see what attracts the most attention.

Rule No. 6. Follow the other ads that are competing with yours, and then *do the opposite.* I had one of my associates in my real estate office run an ad with the headline "OWNER DYING." The second line read: " to sell this lovely three-bedroom home." It may have been in poor taste, but the phones rang off the hook. Many callers began with "I think that ad you ran was disgusting, but while I have you on the phone, tell me more about that house." Tasteless as it was, it got the phones to ring . . . and that's the name of the game.

Rule No. 7. Arrange to be home while your ad is running. If you are not home to answer the phone, you may as well not run the ad.

Rule No. 8. Prepare your response to any callers. You don't want to have a canned speech, but you should know how to give them enough information to arrange a meeting to see the home, if they show any signs of interest.

Rule No. 9. When you get a call, get the caller's name and phone number. Someone who is unwilling to even give you a name is probably not a sincere buyer. You can always say, "I'm on the other line. Can I get your name and number and call you right back?"

USING BROCHURES

If you have a computer, it is easy to use any word-processing program to prepare a one-page brochure telling the facts about your home. Since added words cost you nothing here, use the most descriptive language you can to paint an enticing picture of your home.

Practical Point: You may be a genius when it comes to your command of the English language and vocabulary. Forget it here! Make your ad descriptive but use everyday language and words. To give you an idea, advertising agencies generally state that most ads are written for someone with a third-grade education. Shocking, isn't it!

If you wish, you can paste a photo of the home on the brochure. Take the finished brochure to the nearest quick copy or office supply store and have some photocopied. If you stick with black and white, you can probably get them for as little as four or five cents a copy (about $1 in color). Distribute them to anyone you think may have an interest. When someone calls on your sign or newspaper ad, offer to send a brochure. It's another way of getting a name and address. Make sure you put your address on the brochure.

Important Point: Make sure your yard sign and brochures clearly read "Shown by appointment only" and include your phone number on both. Otherwise, you will have people knocking on your door at all hours.

OTHER ADVERTISING MEDIA

In addition to yard signs and newspaper advertising, there are still some reasonably priced alternatives you can consider to "get the word out." Don't overlook the neighbors who may know of someone looking for a home in your area. There are companies that sell boxes or tubes that attach to your "For Sale" sign in which you can insert copies of your brochure for anyone to stop and take.

USING THE INTERNET TO MARKET YOUR HOME

Internet marketing has become the marketing phenomenon of the late twentieth century. Just about everything and anything is for sale on the Internet including homes.

First of all, in case you are new to the Internet, "search engines" are the various programs that you can use to find almost anything. Among thousands, the main ones are, to name a few, Yahoo, Lycos, Excite, WebCrawler, HotBot, Microsoft Network, Go Network, and Alta Vista. Anyone searching for something on the Internet will use one or more of these search engines.

A point of interest. When you begin your search, you will find all kinds of Web sites appearing that have little or nothing to do with the subject you typed in your search. Don't let this discourage you. Just forge ahead.

If you are on the Internet, try searching for "homes for sale" on one or more of the various search engines. The results will amaze you. We did several searches, trying various ways of locating homes for sale. Let's look at our results on "HotBot," one of the six or seven top search engines. We tried four different ways.

WHAT WE SEARCHED FOR	NUMBER OF WEB SITES FOUND	COMMENTS
For sale by owner	650,200	We did not specify "homes" so our search found everything for sale—boats, cars, etc.
Homes for sale	573,900	This search eliminated everything except homes, but included homes listed by brokers

continued . . .

WHAT WE SEARCHED FOR	NUMBER OF WEB SITES FOUND	COMMENTS
Homes for sale by owner	161,300	These were all homes for sale by owner (no brokers) but included homes from all over the country
Ft. Lauderdale homes for sale by owner	2,000	We narrowed the search to Ft. Lauderdale

As you can see you need to search for specifics in order to make the search meaningful. If we were looking for a product or service on the Internet, and where it was located was not important, we could end up with hundreds of thousands of Web sites dealing with that particular product or service. If you have any experience on the Internet, you know that getting listed and found by visitors is the most difficult task a Web marketer faces. Unless your product or service is listed in the top twenty or thirty on the list, visitors will rarely, if ever, find your site or ad.

Why is this important to you? Many home sellers list their homes themselves on the Internet using the "free Web page" many Internet Service Providers offer when you sign up for their service. It is doubtful that anyone will ever see your "FSBO" ad. Assuming a visitor looks at the first thirty listings on a search, and your home is listing number 123,000, you can see what your chances will be of being seen by visitors.

HOW TO AVOID GETTING LOST ON THE SEARCH ENGINES

There are companies that specialize in listing FSBOs nationwide. Some are large enough to attract listings from nationwide home sellers. Their Web sites list these properties, complete with photos and descriptions, for a modest fee. They break their Web site down further so visitors can search for homes in specific cities and states, and three-bedroom homes, homes with swimming pools, etc., as well.

More important, Internet marketing is their primary function. They devote countless hours and expertise to getting their Web site discovered by visitors. Most of them will continually rank in the top ten or twenty Web sites on all of the major search engines.

Listing your home on the Internet is usually very inexpensive, but don't expect miracles. You may not even get one response. You can, however, use your Internet home listing to your advantage by letting everyone know that your home is listed and where to find it. It will help you eliminate a lot of questions, at least from the callers who use the net. There is also some prestige in being able to say, "I have my home listed on the Internet."

Spend some time looking at various For Sale By Owner Web sites, using different search criteria, such as we did in our example. Try your search on different search engines. Select the ones that appear most often and see how you can list your home with them and what it will cost to do so. You can then select one or more of the most active sites you find.

NOTE: The CD-ROM accompanying this book has lists of FSBO Web sites. You should be able to just click on to visit that site, once you are on line.

CAUTION: Follow the rules of good advertising. Don't give the visitor to your Web page so much information that there is no reason to call you. You can also encourage responses by e-mail to your e-mail address.

Although it is not the best place to expose your home, it is one more interesting and inexpensive approach you can consider. And that's what it is all about.

CHAPTER 4

SHOWING YOUR HOME AND HOLDING AN OPEN HOUSE

Well, your home is ready to show, you have a sign in the front yard, and you have run ads. Now you're all set to greet visitors when they call. What happens now?

The first thing you need to do, after you "sell" them on your home over the phone, is to set up a time for a showing. After you obtain their names, and hopefully their phone numbers, and they express an interest in seeing your home, you give them the address and set up a time for showing. Don't be disappointed if they don't show up. Remember we said that once they know the price and the address, they may drive by and feel it is not worth what you are asking and keep on going. Unfortunately, most of them will not have the courtesy to call and cancel the appointment.

Remember to do the following: Have all the lights on, including closet lights, even if it's a sunny day. Have all the draperies open during the day and closed at night, unless you have a breathtaking view out of your window at night such as a lighted swimming pool and patio area. Make sure everything is picked up and straightened. Have all valuables put safely away. There is no reason to tempt anyone, especially since you don't know who they are. Weather permitting, have the front door open if you have a screen door. Have pets locked outside, if possible. Use the checklist on pages 32-33 to be sure you have covered all the important details.

WELCOMING YOUR POTENTIAL BUYERS

Greet your visitors at the front door. Introduce yourself and invite them in. Ask them to sign your guest register (which you want to have for follow-up calls in case you change the price or terms on your property). Your guest register can be a simple note pad with name and address headings.

Stay with your visitors as you direct them on a guided tour of your home. Avoid saying such lame things as "This is the kitchen." You can be certain they will recognize it as a kitchen as soon as they enter the room. Instead tell them how great a kitchen it is. "Look at that beautiful view out of the window over the sink. It almost makes dishwashing enjoyable." Or, "That is a new, state-of-the-art microwave and browner. It cooks great meals."

Focus on the positive. There is an old song, "Accentuate the Positive and Eliminate the Negative," that fits here. As you show your home, you want to accentuate its positive features. Verbally "move your guests into the home." Although you cannot "eliminate the negative," you can minimize it by talking about the positive features. You know where your home has shortcomings. Be prepared to answer questions about them. Don't assume that if you just ignore them, they will go away. For example, you know the closet in the second bedroom is very small and you can be sure you'll regularly hear adverse comments about it. Counter with something like, "I agree. We had the same reservations when we first looked at the house but, as you can see, our daughter has a lot of clothing hanging in there and there is still room. We haven't had any space problems." Continue leading your prospects through the home, pointing out all its features. Make sure you keep track of everyone in your home. Don't let someone wander off into another room, if you can avoid it. It's your home and you have a right to control where your visitors go.

Most prospects are making the rounds of several houses before making a decision to buy. Rarely will you be able to convince someone to enter into a contract on the first visit. Be sure to leave the door open for a return visit and another look. Offer a flyer or brochure to be taken after the visit.

HINT: If a potential buyer does come back a second time and walk around the house discussing how to arrange the furniture in it, you have a live one. Now is the time to work on a contract. We'll discuss this subject in detail in Chapter 7.

HOW TO HOLD AN OPEN HOUSE

Now that you've had some experience in showing your home, your next step will be to hold an Open House.

The first step is getting ready. Begin by running an ad telling of the Open House, and now you must include the address in the ad. Spell out the exact hours and day you will have it open to visitors (Sunday from 1:00 P.M. to 5:00 P.M.). You can expect visitors to be there before the scheduled time; if you are ready for them, let them in.

Have your home ready, with lights on, toilet lids down, quiet music playing, etc. Park your cars across the street or in a neighbor's driveway. Leave your driveway open for visitor parking. Your front yard sign should also announce the Open House. Have a separate sign for this purpose that can be removed as soon as the hours end. You should also have directional signs to your property. If you have to make a couple of turns off the main road, place a directional sign at each intersection showing visitors which way to turn.

Important Point: Check with your local sign ordinance department of the city to see what, if any, restrictions there may be regarding placement of signs.

Have a list of other homes that have sold in the area (you know how to get one now) and a list of those for sale in the neighborhood and how they compare with yours. If your home shows very favorably compared with others, hand out a copy of the list with your home at the top.

You must keep control of traffic through your home. It may be advisable to have both you and your spouse present to escort guests.

Make sure each guest signs in. That will help screen out anyone who is not really interested. Use the checklist on pages 32–33 to help you keep track of the details.

Several brokers will probably show up. Collect business cards from each of them. Most will volunteer to give you one before you ask. This is also your chance to see which brokers you really like in case you later decide to list with one of them. They all have an edge over their fellow associates. They took the time to visit your Open House. (Probably to try to get a listing . . . but they did show up.)

Thank everyone for coming. Make sure all the guests have one of your brochures when they leave. If they decide they have no interest in your home, they may know someone who does and hand over your brochure. Conversely, they just might go home and take another look at the brochure and consider your home a possibility.

Once your Open House has ended, be sure to collect all of your signs and store them for the next one. Once everything is back to normal, you can sit down and relax.

Holding an Open House is not an easy task. Not only do you have to prepare for it and advertise, but you have to be on your toes at all times. You have a four-hour selling job to do. Since it's your home, and you know it better than anyone else, selling the features should be easy.

Important Point: Don't "oversell" your home. It will be a turnoff if a visitor thinks you are pushing hard. Brokers face this problem constantly when a buyer assumes the broker will sell anything just to make a commission. Since you have only one house to sell, potential buyers become gun-shy even more quickly when pushed. They figure you are anxious to sell and will either run or make a low-ball offer.

You must also keep track of your visitors to make certain none are helping themselves to small valuable objects that you may have forgotten to put safely away. This point is so important to remember that it is repeated several times in this text.

Checklist for Preparing Your Home for Showing

With buyers, first impressions count. A small investment in time and money will give your home an edge over other listings in the area when the time comes to show it to a prospective buyer. Here are some suggestions that will help you to get top market value:

General Maintenance
Oil squeaky doors
Tighten doorknobs
Replace burned-out lights
Clean and repair windows
Touch up chipped paint
Repair leaking taps and toilets

Cleanliness
Shampoo carpets
Clean washer, dryer and tubs
Clean refrigerator and stove
Clean and freshen bathrooms
Clean other areas from smudges, etc.

The First Impression
Clean and tidy entrance
Make sure doorbell works
Polish door hardware
Walk around your home
  as a potential buyer . . .
What is *your* first impression
  of it?

Outside
Cut lawns
Trim shrubs and lawns
Weed and edge gardens
Clear walk and driveway of
  leaves
Repair gutters and eaves
Touch up exterior paint

Creating Atmosphere
Turn on all lights, even in
  day time
Open drapes in the daytime
Play quiet background
  music
Keep pets outdoors

Looking "Big"
Clear stairs and halls
Store excess furniture
Make closets neat and tidy
Clear counters and stove

Checklist for Holding an Open House

An Open House is a good way to attract visitors to the home. If you are a broker, it is a good way to pick up prospects. (Sellers, don't pay attention to that comment.) Seller or listing broker, here is a list of how to prepare the home for an Open House.

____ Park your car in front. Make the home look occupied.

____ Make sure yard, driveway and walkways are clear and clean.

____ Make sure the house is clean and free from clutter.

____ Open all draperies, blinds, etc., in the daytime.

____ Close all draperies, blinds, etc., at night (unless the yard features lighted patio and gardens or something worth seeing at night).

____ Have brochures (preferably color with photos) on the kitchen counter to hand out.

____ Have a supply of your business cards ready to hand out.

____ Turn on all the lights, even in the daytime, including bathrooms and closets.

____ If a closet is extra large and neat, have the door open.

____ Have a guest registration book easily available for guests.

____ Close toilet lids.

____ Have background music playing.

____ Have a faint aroma of a pleasant smell in the room, especially the kitchen. Vanilla or cinnamon is good. Don't make it strong and do not use a perfume or deodorizer smell.

____ Make sure the owner's valuables are safely put away.

____ Make sure all sinks are clean and shiny.

____ Have directional signs to the property with an "Open" sign in front.

continued . . .

____ Have a list of homes for sale in the neighborhood. (You know any visitor will be checking them out anyway. Be prepared to answer any questions about them and how they compare with yours.)

____ Have a thorough knowledge of the home you are holding open. If you can't sell it, who can?

____ Make personal contact with every visitor (if possible). Answer questions; get them to sign a guest register or information card. You want their names, addresses, phone numbers and what interest they might have in buying a home. (If you are a broker, you might have a list of prospects to buy or sell a home.)

CHAPTER 5

PRESENTING THE OFFER-TO-SELL-AND-PURCHASE CONTRACT

Once you reach the point of seriously advertising for buyers for your home, you need to have a contract ready to present to a potential buyer. We mentioned earlier that a prospect who comes back a second (or third) time is ready to buy. This is especially true of someone who is verbally arranging furniture in your home. What do you do now? You now switch from being a homeowner to being a salesperson. Use open-ended comments like "It sounds like you have some interesting ideas for decorating" or "What do you intend to do with the spare bedroom?" Try to avoid questions with a simple "yes" or "no" answer. The more the person talks, and the more you lead that person into a "I want this home" frame of mind, the easier it is to suggest an offer to purchase. The buyer may not be willing to sit down with you and sign a contract, but with sufficient motivation, it just might happen.

Many buyers will not commit to you at this time. If they are serious enough to make an offer, they are smart not to tell you anyway because they will probably have their attorney draw up the offer. (We discuss this subject in the "buyer" section.) All you can do at this point is convince them that your home is the one they want. Don't be surprised or disappointed if a contract never comes in and the couple you thought was ready to buy never contacts you again. Welcome to the real estate business! Generally, what happens, as we discuss throughout this book with both buyer and seller, is that they get cold feet or have second thoughts.

I had a fifty-year-old man come into my office one morning in tears. He and his wife had been up all night because they had entered into a contract to purchase a home the evening before and now felt they had made a tremendous mistake. (We arranged to get them out of the contract without any costs.) It's like an impulse purchase.

However, home buying takes a little more thought and effort than ordering merchandise on the Internet. All you can hope is that, if you have sincere buyers, they will be sufficiently impressed with your home to keep that "impulse" thought going until they get a contract prepared.

Although a potential buyer may not be ready to buy instantly, you need to have a contract ready to sign, after you fill it out, just in case. Since every state has its own laws of what is acceptable, it is impossible to cover all aspects of a Sale and Purchase Contract here. On page 50, you will see a complete sample contract that will meet most of the requirements. (You may want to pick up a copy of an acceptable contract if the one we've included definitely will not work in your area.) As a practical matter, a contract is a written document that is agreed to and executed by the parties involved. Using this "loose" interpretation, a sheet of notebook paper, with all the details handwritten, could be used as a legally binding contract. I'm not suggesting this should be done, but as long as the parties to the document agree to what is written on it, it would probably hold up in a court of law.

Important Point: NEVER enter any type of a legally binding document without the advice of legal counsel, if there is some question about the intent of the parties. Once a contract is executed by all parties, you could be forced to live with it.

Always spell out every item in detail in the contract. If the item is already pre-printed, but not detailed enough, add to it. It may prevent a problem later. As the homeowner, you have more leeway than a broker will have; you may be able to get by using a generic contract.

WHAT'S IN A CONTRACT

Let's briefly discuss the contract itself. At first glance, it may look overwhelming, but there are really only a few basic sections. The first is the heading that spells out who the buyer and seller are. Next, the contract lists the name, address and legal description of the property. (The legal description is the way your property is listed in the tax rolls and property records. It usually consists of a description like: "Lot 3, block 6 of section 32 hometown estates 43-54.") The property will also contain a folio number, which is a lengthy, second identifying number. You can usually find both forms of identification on your deed, mortgage documents and real estate tax bill. Every parcel of land in the nation has a unique legal description similar to the above example. Some descriptions can be much longer than our example. This section of our contract will also include a list of any personal property being conveyed with the transfer of title. Personal property is anything that is not considered "attached to and part of" the actual home. If the box on the contract is not large enough for the list, an addendum can be attached to and become a part of the contract. The fact that an addendum is attached with a list of personal property will be noted in the property description box. There may also be a list of personal property that is not included in the sale, in case there are items that could be questioned later.

The next section of most contracts spells out the offering price being made on the property, and the terms and conditions of the financing. It will state how much cash is being deposited with the contract.

Important Point: Ideally, you want at least a ten percent deposit with a contract. An attorney, Title Company or other neutral party should hold that deposit in escrow. It cannot be released from escrow except at the closing of title or, if the contract falls apart, only by consent of both parties to the transaction. In most cases, the buyer will not have the full ten percent deposit sitting in a checking account, and so may offer a check for, say one thousand dollars, with the balance of the ten percent due within the next two or three business days or once the contract is agreed to and executed by both parties. The remainder of this section of the contract spells out the terms and conditions of the financing. That includes any mortgage that is being assumed, any new mortgage that is being applied for and/or any mortgage the buyer wants the seller to carry.

The next clause is time limit for acceptance. You must spell out a time limit for the buyer to make a decision and return an executed contract. The expected date of closing will also be spelled out on the contract.

The remainder of the contract, until you reach the signature page, spells out all of the terms, conditions and disclosures that are made by the seller and agreed to by the buyer. Space does not permit covering each of them. Most are self-explanatory. The remainder of this chapter will be devoted to covering the most important clauses that are often ignored or, in many cases, not already pre-printed in the contract. We'll explain each of them and why they are important to include in your contract. (A sample contract can be found at the end of this chapter, beginning on page 50.)

TERMS AND CONDITIONS

Most offer-to-purchase contracts are filled with "stock" terms and conditions. Here are a few that are most important, some of which are not generally on a pre-printed contract form. By the way, most stationery stores carry blank home purchase contract forms.

Documents: Seller's attorney, or other closing agent, will prepare the deed, no-lien affidavit, seller-held mortgage (if any), bill of sale for personal property, and will insure that a clear and marketable title to the property is given.

Mortgage Recording: Seller will generally pay to have a mortgage he or she is carrying recorded at the courthouse. It is vitally important to have this done as quickly after closing as possible.

Taxes: Seller is responsible for real estate taxes up until the day of closing.

Escrow Account: The buyer owes the seller for the balance in the escrow account, if the buyer is assuming the present mortgage where the escrow account is held.

Liens: Certified and confirmed liens, as of the day of closing, are the responsibility of the seller. Pending liens not yet on the books are generally the responsibility of the buyer.

Fire or Other Casualty: All contracts spell out the seller's and buyer's liability and course of action in the event the property is damaged prior to closing.

Property Maintenance: The seller is expected to maintain the property in the same condition it was in when the contract was executed.

Withholding Payment: A clause will specify how money will be escrowed to cover the cost of any agreed-upon repairs by the seller, if they are not completed by the day of closing.

Remedies for Default: If either buyer or seller defaults, the remedy is spelled out in the contract.

Inspections: Time limits are set for any inspections that were agreed to. As inspections are completed, that contingency should be removed by written notice to the seller. *Buyer cannot back out of the contract without "just cause."*

Repair Limits: Most contracts spell out how much repair cost the seller is obligated to pay. This cost could be in at least three areas: Roof, Termite, and General Repairs. *Quite often, the form contract will have a percentage of the purchase price amount written in for each item. Be certain you understand and agree to these terms; they are negotiable.* You may not want to be liable for 3% of the purchase price for each—roof repairs, termite damage and general repairs. This would amount to 9% of the purchase price or $15,750 on a $175,000 home. You can expect the buyer to want to collect as much as possible.

PROVIDING FOR CONTINGENCIES

There are many other clauses in a contract. *Many of them will be added to protect the buyer.* The buyer must have an "out" in the event there are problems that cannot be resolved. The two most common are:

1. The buyer does not qualify for a mortgage and therefore cannot afford to buy your home. Your new mortgage clause should spell out terms stating *that if the buyer is unable to obtain a mortgage, after making reasonable efforts in applying and qualifying for a mortgage, the contract will be null and void, the deposit refunded to the buyer and liability on all parties shall cease.* The wording must be such to require the buyer to make an honest effort in applying for and trying to qualify for the mortgage.

2. The same condition holds true for inspections. The contract spells out a certain percentage or dollar amount that will be allowed for repairs, but what happens if the inspector determines the building needs a new roof, or heating and air conditioning system (the old one is not working and cannot be repaired) or there is severe settling and signs that it will continue to do so. These repairs could cost several times the allowance in the contract. What happens then? In this case, unless the buyer and seller can agree on a revised repair allowance figure, the buyer should have the right to back out of the contract without penalty. If you are unsure of the legality of your contract form or how to protect yourself when preparing a contract, check with your legal counsel for help.

Sometimes buyers submit an offer to purchase contingent upon their selling and closing on their home before they close on yours. This can be a real problem for you. You think your home is sold, you enter into a contract to purchase another one and suddenly the buyer backs out because her home has not sold. Although you can take a backup contract, in the event the primary one does not close, this will not satisfy most buyers. A buyer who is ready to buy now wants to have a definite closing agreement on your home. Providing a potential buyer with a backup contract that may or may not be valid in a month or two will usually terminate that relationship. If a potential buyer already has a binding contract on her home, your position may be a little stronger. You still want to know that all contingencies on that contract have been satisfied and just a closing date is needed. Even then, there is always a chance that the sale will still fall apart and you will be left with a home that has been taken off the market for a month or more and still has not been sold.

BROKER DATA

The next section generally spells out the terms, conditions and names of any real estate brokers who are involved in the transaction, if any.

SIGN HERE

Finally, the contract has the signature lines for buyer(s) and seller(s) with the date signed, their social security numbers and addresses. The date signed is important if there happens to be more than one offer on the property in front of you at the same time. You will know which one was submitted first. This generally is not important because you will be selecting the better of the two offers anyway.

> **NOTE:** Unless the contract comes in at full asking price with no contingencies, you always have the option to counteroffer. You may look over the contract and decide that the offering price of $150,000 is unacceptable. You may negotiate a little but a $25,000 reduction from your asking price may be ridiculous. This holds true for any other terms written into the contract that are asking you for more than you are willing to offer. At this point, you determine what you will accept and make changes in the contract accordingly. We'll cover this in detail later.

POINT NO. 1. Sellers almost always list the price higher than they expect to obtain.

POINT NO. 2. Buyers know this and expect to negotiate on price and terms!

CONTRACT CAVEATS

Check, or have your attorney check, all of the fine print in the contract. There could be something pre-printed in the basic contract that is not desirable. It goes without saying that you should carefully check everything that has been written into the contract by the buyer.

Important Point: Anything written into a contract supercedes what is pre-printed in the contract.

For example, it may be pre-printed in a contract that the seller agrees to pay up to one or two percent of the purchase price for any repairs that may be needed. The buyer, however, has a statement in the addendum to the contract that states, "The seller agrees, at his cost, to replace the roof prior to closing, with the same quality of materials and workmanship that is customary and standard for the area." Now we have a question that needs to be resolved before you accept the contract. Does the cost of a new roof eliminate or supercede the pre-printed repair clause or is it in addition to that clause? You could be facing considerable expense you had not planned on. It is in your best interest to make the cost of replacing the roof as all or part of that repair clause.

HANDLING MULTIPLE OFFERS

You have your home on the market and suddenly you have two offer-to-purchase contracts come in on the same day. Now what do you do?

You're probably thinking, "I should be so lucky," but it does happen. This is especially true if you have your home priced at fair market value and are in a seller's market. Here are some guidelines for handling this "problem."

1. The first thing you want to do is inform both parties that you have a second offer and you will be reviewing both of them.

2. You also want to allow sufficient time to make a selection and work at pulling the first one together into a firm purchase contract. Your goal is to keep both offers active until you get one of them firm. You will probably have to get some additional negotiating time with both buyers. If the first one does not "fly," you still have the second one to work with.

    You've heard the term "time is of the essence." This means it is important to get the contract resolved as quickly as possible. This is especially true in this case. You cannot expect either buyer to wait around until you spend a few days deciding which offer is the better one. Remember, a buyer can withdraw a contract at any time, prior to acceptance. If one buyer decides not to wait, you are left with only one . . . and it may end up not being the better of the two.

3. Examine each offer carefully. Do not look just at the price being offered. The highest price offer may be the least desirable one. Here is what you need to check:

   - Offering price. All else being equal, you obviously want to choose the one that will give you the most money.

   - The financing terms. Perhaps the buyer with the best price offer is also looking for 95 or 100% financing, and/or may also be looking for a below-market interest rate or some other terms that may be impossible to obtain.

   - Other terms and conditions written in the contract such as: Inspection clauses and how much you will be expected to pay for repair work that may be needed.

   - Closing date. Can you live with the closing date the buyer is requesting? Is it too short a time to allow you to close on another home, pack and move?

     Conversely, is it too long a time? You may have already found the home you want and have a contract on it, with a bridge loan. (Bridge loans are discussed elsewhere in this book.) The buyer may want a three-month closing, so you will be stuck with mortgage payments on your present home plus payments on the bridge loan for the new home. In effect, you will be making double mortgage payments during the period of time until your present home sale closes.

   - What does the buyer want to have included in the sale? (Personal property, etc.)

   - How large a deposit should be included with the contract? You want at least ten percent of the purchase price as a deposit. We have already discussed that a minimum deposit is usually acceptable with the initial offer to purchase. Once the contract is agreed to, and executed by all parties, an added deposit should be added by the buyer to bring the total amount to ten percent of the purchase price. The reason is simple. Someone may be willing to put up two hundred dollars to tie up your home under a contract. In the meantime, the buyer may continue looking, find a home preferable to yours, and enter into a purchase contract on that one, too. If the second home is purchased, you have just tied up your property for a month or more with nothing to show for it, except the two hundred dollars the buyer was willing to sacrifice. Sure, you may be able to sue for "specific performance" if you want to expend the time and money to do it. That will also tie up your home for a few more months. It usually is not worth the effort and you end up taking your property off the market until the problem is resolved. This often results in a greater loss than just letting the buyer out of the contract and going on with the process of selling your home.

- You need to compare the two buyers. Which one is better financially able to buy your home? This is where being pre-qualified for a mortgage can be so important. If you know one of the buyers already has a mortgage commitment and is financially capable of buying your home, this is a great asset for both the buyer and seller.

The important point here is to examine all parts of a purchase contract, including the buyer's qualifications. Don't just pick the one with the highest offering price. It may be the least desirable contract or the one least likely to close.

ACCEPTING THE OFFER

Once you select the better of the two contracts, you want to concentrate on that one. Get all points of discussion or disagreement satisfied as quickly as possible. Have any changes to the original contract written in and initialed by all parties. (We discuss this in detail in the section on contract negotiation.) Once you have a firm, executed contract in your hands, with the added deposit, you need to inform the second buyer that you have accepted the first contract.

WHAT TO DO IF A SECOND CONTRACT COMES IN A DAY LATER

So far, we've discussed how to handle two contracts that come in at the same time. What do you do if you are already negotiating on one contract and a second one comes in a day or two later? Even worse, the second contract is better than the one you are already negotiating.

You can explain the situation to the first buyer, assuming you have not yet committed to anything. If, however, you have made a counter offer, with your changes initialed and the contract signed, you are committed to that contract. If the buyer accepts the changes, you have a firm purchase contract. You need to let the second buyer know that the home is now under contract.

Don't Get into a Bidding Contest

One sure-fire way to lose both contracts is to try and work one contract against the other. "If you increase your price by $5,000, I'll take your contract." Then to the second buyer you make a similar offer. Once the two buyers realize you are bidding one against the other, you will probably lose both of them . . . not to mention the negative reputation you will have in the home seller marketplace . . . and word does spread.

Offer a Backup Contract

Don't eliminate the "runner-up" in your two-contract offer from the contest. Suggest that the contract be left with you as a backup contract. In the event the first one falls apart, the second will be in first position to buy your home. This often keeps a buyer on the hook and gives you the security of knowing your home will be sold to one or the other.

Unfortunately, a homebuyer who needs to buy a house cannot always wait to see if yours becomes available. If you find yourself in a seller's market, this idea will work better than in a buyer's market where a lot of homes are for sale. I've seen cases in my office where a property was "hot" enough that we had as many as two or three backup contracts on it.

Set a Time Limit for Acceptance

In order to insure that you get at least one of your multiple offers to the contract stage, you need to have a time limit for acceptance on each offer. If you allow a week or two to have a contract counter offer accepted, you will not be able to keep that backup buyer waiting. Both buyer and seller should want a time limit for acceptance. The seller wants it to get the deal under contract as quickly as possible because buyers often get buyer's remorse while waiting for a contract to be approved and will frequently withdraw it. Once all parties execute the contract, the buyer will generally lose that "Am I doing the right thing" syndrome.

Likewise, the buyer will want a time limit for acceptance of an offer to prevent the seller from having time to "shop" the contract. What does that mean? A seller who is fortunate enough to have two people who both want the home will sometimes show a second potential buyer the contract already in hand. "Here is an offer for $150,000 I have right now. If you want to beat that offer, I'll consider your contract first." Don't fall into this trap. We have already mentioned the likely consequences of getting into a bidding contest.

Having more than one offer to consider is ideal, but you must handle all offers fairly for both you and the potential buyers. Above all, make your decisions timely and keep both buyers informed as to where they stand.

THE IMPORTANCE OF A WRITTEN INVENTORY

Once a buyer is ready to submit an offer to purchase, you need to prepare a written inventory of what stays with the home at closing and what you, as the seller, intend to remove and take with you. The two parties can certainly negotiate what stays and what goes, but once agreement is reached, put it in writing. Both you and the buyer need to review this written inventory list, *sign it,* and attach it so that it becomes a part of the sales contract. You may want to state: "An inventory of personal property, included with the sale of this property, is attached to and a part of this contract." Label it "Exhibit A" and refer to it as such. Once that inventory has been negotiated and agreed to in writing, stick to it. Don't decide at the last minute, "Oh, I think I want to take that one light fixture." You can be certain the buyer, during the final walkthrough on the day of closing, will notice it has been removed, even if you replaced it with a similar one.

This simple procedure will eliminate confusion and arguments later. Verbal agreements may work on the day they are agreed to, but over time, memories fade and what was agreed to a few weeks earlier is misunderstood, or intentionally and conveniently forgotten.

PREPARING THE INVENTORY

You, as the seller, need to prepare a formal *written* inventory of the personal property that is included in the sale. First, let's define "personal property." In the strict sense of the word, anything that is not permanently attached to the walls, ceiling, floors etc., is considered personal property. These common problems emphasize the need for a written inventory.

You may have a certain item in the home, such as a crystal chandelier, that is an heirloom, has sentimental value, or is valuable and not normally found in a home. You want to take it with you to your new home. You must make it clear to a buyer, when the home is first shown, what is not included in the sale. It's much easier to reach an agreement before the buyer decides to make an offer. Make sure you put it in writing.

Quite often, you may decide you want something that is really attached and you decide, perhaps at the last minute, to take it. This can cause problems. Take a look at this situation from the point of view of a buyer who likes your home and is ready to enter into an offer-to-purchase contract. The buyer likes the room layout and sizes, the neighborhood, the modern kitchen with a view of the spacious yard, the "Hunter" ceiling fans in each room, etc. Oops, you intended to take those Hunter fans so you replace them with the inexpensive $35.00 each variety. On the day of the closing, the buyer does a final walkthrough inspection of the property and the first thing noticed is that the ceiling fans are different. We have a problem here. At best, you will have to reimburse the buyer for the value of the fans that should have been left in the first place. The worst scenario is that the buyer gets mad and walks out on the closing. I've seen this happen on the most unimportant items.

Unfortunately, they were important to the buyer and seller. Back when every home had a TV antenna on the roof, one seller decided to remove it and take it with him. That closing actually fell apart because the buyer refused to close unless it was replaced and the seller refused. I even offered to pay the $50 to replace it, but at this point it was a matter of principle between the two and neither would give in. In another case, a buyer fell in love with a toilet seat printed with big red roses. The seller removed it and almost lost the sale unless he replaced the seat.

QUESTIONS TO CONSIDER

You should settle the following property issues and reflect them in your inventory statement.

- It's Mine, but I Don't Want It. I'd Like to Leave It. This is fine, if the buyer does want the item. If not, someone has to pay to get rid of it. It may be a large, old TV set that doesn't work or a rusty playground swing set that the children outgrew ten years ago. The buyer may expect to either have it removed before closing or have you pay to have it removed. Resolve how the property will be disposed of and who will be responsible.

- What About Appliances? Some items, such as washing machines, dryers and refrigerators, may or may not be attached, in the strict sense of the word. Washing machines are "attached" by water lines and sewer lines. Refrigerators may have an icemaker water line "attached." Again, it is up to you and the buyer to agree to what must be left in the home and what you can take.

- So, What's Personal Property and What's Not? In the strict meaning of the words, personal property is anything that is not physically attached to the home. Now comes an interesting question. The draperies are not attached. Can you take them? The answer is usually "yes," even though it may cause a problem. As a practical matter, why take them if it is going to cause a potential problem? Remember, we are trying to insure that the sale closes. How important are those draperies if they could kill the sale?

SELLING YOUR FURNISHINGS

Quite often a buyer falls in love with a home, partly because of the home itself and partly because of the way it is furnished. The seller is approached to see if he or she will sell certain pieces of furniture, or all of it, to the buyer.

The sale of personal property has nothing to do with the sale of the home. Any agreement to sell furnishings must be a separate agreement, in writing, between the buyer and seller. The seller will furnish the buyer with a "bill of sale" for the inventory of items to be included on the list of furnishings. Do not try to make the sale of furniture part of the contract to purchase the home. You're asking for trouble. Either the buyer or seller may experience a change of heart prior to closing and, if that inventory is part of the contract on the sale of the home, the whole transaction may be lost. The sale of the personal property is, and should be, a separate and private transaction between the two parties. There may also be the question of capital gains tax due on the personal property if its value was added to the purchase price of the home.

You may think we put a lot of emphasis on this subject, but you would be amazed at how often minor disagreements on items that have nothing to do with the home sale itself can create a problem on or before the closing date. Don't let this happen to you. As we pointed out before, it is much easier to get parties to agree during the initial negotiation stage of a contract than it is to make changes after the contract has been executed by all parties.

Sample Real Estate Sale and Purchase Contract

_____, of _____ as Seller,

and _____, of _____ as
Buyer, hereby agree that the Seller shall sell and the Buyer shall buy the following
described property UPON THE TERMS AND CONDITIONS HEREINAFTER SET
FORTH, which shall include the STANDARDS FOR REAL ESTATE TRANSACTIONS set
forth within this contract.

1. **LEGAL DESCRIPTION** of real estate located in _____
County, State of _____ together with all improvements and attached
items, including fixtures, built-in appliances, attached wall-to-wall carpeting, draperies,
rods and window coverings. The other items included in the purchase price are:
_____The
following items are excluded from the purchase:_____

2. **PURCHASE PRICE** $ _____ Dollars.
Method of Payment:

(a) Deposit to be held in trust by: $

    _____   _____

(b) Additional Deposit due within _____ days $ _____

(c) Approximate principal balance of first
     mortgage to which conveyance shall be
     subject, if any, to Mortgage Lender: $
Interest _____ % per annum:
     Method of payment: _____

(d) Other_____ $ _____

(e) Balance to close with cashier's check. $ _____

continued . . .

3. **FINANCING:** If the purchase price or any part of it is to be financed by a third-party loan, this Contract is conditioned on Buyer obtaining a written commitment within _____ days after Effective Date for (CHECK ONLY ONE): _____a fixed; _____an adjustable; or _____ a fixed or adjustable rate loan for the principal amount of $ _____, at an initial interest rate not to exceed _____%, and a term of _____ years. Buyer will make application within _____ days after Effective Date and use reasonable diligence to obtain the loan commitment and, there after, to satisfy the terms and conditions of the commitment and close the loan. Buyer shall pay all loan expenses. If Buyer fails to obtain the commitment under this subparagraph within the time for the commitment of the terms and conditions of the commitment, then either party, by written notice to the other, may cancel this Contract and Buyer shall be refunded the deposit(s).

4. **CLOSING DATE:** This contract shall be closed and the deed and possession shall be delivered on or before the _____ ____A.M. ____P.M., on the _____ day of _____, _____, unless extended by other provisions of this contract.

5. **PRORATIONS:** Taxes, insurance, interest, rents and other expenses and revenue of said property shall be prorated as of the date of closing.

6. **PLACE OF CLOSING:** Closing shall be held at the office of the Seller's attorney or as otherwise agreed upon.

7. **TIME IS OF THE ESSENCE:** Time is of the essence for this Sale and Purchase Agreement.

Buyer (___) (___) and Seller (___) (___) acknowledge receipt of a copy of this page, which is page 1 of 4 pages.

continued . . .

8.   RESTRICTIONS, EASEMENTS, LIMITATIONS: Buyer shall take title subject to: (a) Zoning, restrictions, prohibitions and requirements imposed by governmental authority, (b) Restrictions and matters appearing on the plat or common to the subdivision, (c) Public utility easements of record, provided said easements are located on the side or rear lines of the property, (d) Taxes for year of closing, assumed mortgages, and purchase money mortgages, if any, (e) Other: _____. Seller warrants that there shall be no violations of building or zoning codes at the time of closing.

9.   DEFAULT BY BUYER: If Buyer fails to perform any of the covenants of this contract, all money paid pursuant to this contract by Buyer as aforesaid shall be retained by or for the account of the Seller as consideration for the execution of this contract and as agreed liquidated damages and in full settlement of any claims for damages.

10.   DEFAULT BY SELLER: If the Seller fails to perform any of the covenants of this contract, the aforesaid money paid by the Buyer, at the option of the Buyer, shall be returned to the Buyer on demand; or the Buyer shall have only the right of specific performance.

11.   TERMITE INSPECTION: At least 15 days before closing, Buyer, at Buyer's expense, shall have the right to obtain a written report from a licensed exterminator stating that there is no evidence of live termite or other wood-boring insect infestation on said property nor substantial damage from prior infestation on said property. If there is such evidence, Seller shall pay up to three (3%) percent of the purchase price for the treatment required to remedy such infestation, including repairing and replacing portions of said improvements which have been damaged; but if the costs for such treatment or repairs exceed three (3%) percent of the purchase price, Buyer may elect to pay such excess. If Buyer elects not to pay, Seller may pay the excess or cancel the contract.

12.   ROOF INSPECTION: At least 15 days before closing, Buyer, at Buyer's expense, shall have the right to obtain a written report from a licensed roofer stating that the

continued . . .

roof is in a watertight condition. In the event repairs are required either to correct leaks or to replace damage to fascia or soffit, Seller shall pay up to three (3%) percent of the purchase price for said repairs which shall be performed by a licensed roofing contractor; but if the costs for such repairs exceed three (3%) percent of the purchase price, Buyer may elect to pay such excess. If Buyer elects not to pay, Seller may pay the excess or cancel the contract.

13. OTHER INSPECTIONS: At least 15 days before closing, Buyer or his agent may inspect all appliances, air conditioning and heating systems, electrical systems, plumbing, machinery, sprinklers and pool system included in the sale. Seller shall pay for repairs necessary to place such items in working order at the time of closing. Within 48 hours before closing, Buyer shall be entitled, upon reasonable notice to Seller, to inspect the premises to determine that said items are in working order. All items of personal property included in the sale shall be transferred by Bill of Sale with warranty of title.

14. MECHANICS' LIENS: Seller shall furnish to Buyer an affidavit that there have been no improvements to the subject property for 90 days immediately preceding the date of closing, and no financing statements, claims of lien or potential liens known to Seller. If the property has been improved within that time, Seller shall deliver releases or waivers of all mechanics' liens as executed by general contractors, subcontractors, suppliers and material men, in addition to the Seller's lien affidavit, setting forth the names of all general contractors, subcontractors, suppliers and material men and reciting that all bills for work to the subject property which could serve as basis for mechanics' liens have been paid or will be paid at closing time.

Buyer (__) (__) and Seller (__) (__) acknowledge receipt of a copy of this page, which is page 2 of 4 pages.

continued . . .

15. DOCUMENTS FOR CLOSING: Seller's attorney shall prepare deed, note, mortgage, Seller's affidavit, any corrective instruments required for perfecting the title, and closing statement and submit copies of same to Buyer's attorney, and copy of closing statement to the broker, at least two days prior to scheduled closing date.

16. EXPENSES: State documentary stamps required on the instrument of conveyance and the cost of recording any corrective instruments shall be paid by the Seller. Documentary stamps to be affixed to the note secured by the purchase money mortgage, intangible tax on the mortgage, and the cost of recording the deed and purchasing money mortgage shall be paid by the Buyer.

17. INSURANCE: If insurance is to be prorated, the Seller shall on or before the closing date, furnish to Buyer all insurance policies or copies thereof.

18. RISK OF LOSS: If the improvements are damaged by fire or casualty before delivery of the deed and can be restored to substantially the same condition as now within a period of 60 days thereafter, Seller shall so restore the improvements and the closing date and date of delivery of possession hereinbefore provided shall be extended accordingly. If Seller fails to do so, the Buyer shall have the option of (1) taking the property as is, together with insurance proceeds, if any, or (2) canceling the contract, and all deposits shall be forthwith returned to the Buyer and all parties shall be released of any and all obligations and liability.

19. MAINTENANCE: Between the date of the contract and the date of closing, the property, including lawn, shrubbery and pool, if any, shall be maintained by the Seller in the condition as it existed as of the date of the contract, ordinary wear and tear excepted.

20. LEASES: Seller, not less than 15 days before closing, shall furnish to Buyer copies of all written leases and estoppel letters from each tenant specifying the nature and duration of the tenant's occupancy, rental rates and advanced rent and security deposits paid by tenant. If Seller is unable to obtain such letters from tenants, Seller

continued . . .

shall furnish the same information to Buyer within said time period in the form of a Seller's affidavit, and Buyer may contact tenants thereafter to confirm such information. At closing, Seller shall deliver and assign all original leases to Buyer.

21. **OTHER AGREEMENTS:** No agreements or representations, unless incorporated in this contract, shall be binding upon any of the parties.

22. **RADON GAS DISCLOSURE:** Radon is a naturally occurring radioactive gas that, when it has accumulated in a building in sufficient quantities, may present health risks to persons who are exposed to it over time. Levels of radon that exceed Federal and State guidelines have been found in Florida buildings. Additional information regarding radon and radon testing may be obtained from your county public health unit. Buyer may, within the inspection period, have a licensed person test the property for radon. If radon exceeds the accepted level, seller may choose to reduce the level to an acceptable EPA level or either party may cancel the contract if the Seller fails to comply.

23. **LEAD PAINT HAZARD:** Every purchaser of any interest in residential real property on which a residential dwelling was built prior to 1978 is notified that such property may present exposure to lead from lead-based paint that may place young children at risk of developing lead poisoning. Lead poisoning in young children may produce permanent neurological damage, including learning disabilities, reduced intelligence quotient, behavioral problems and impaired memory. Lead poisoning also poses a particular risk to pregnant women. The Seller of any interest in residential real estate is required to provide the Buyer with any information on lead-based paint hazards from risk assessments or inspection in the Seller's possession and notify the Buyer of any known lead-based paint hazards. A risk assessment or inspection for possible lead-based paint hazards is recommended prior to purchase.

Buyer (___) (___) and Seller (___) (___) acknowledge receipt of a copy of this page, which is page 3 of 4 pages.

continued . . .

24. **TYPEWRITTEN OR HANDWRITTEN PROVISIONS:** Typewritten or handwritten provisions inserted in this form shall control all printed provisions in conflict therewith.

25. **SPECIAL CLAUSES:** _____

_____

26. The Following Addenda shall be attached to and become part of this contract:

_____

RIDERS: Check those that apply and are attached to this contract:
____Condominium Rider; ____Lead Paint Disclosure; ____Agency Disclosure (brokers);
____"As Is" Rider; ____Other _____
DISCLOSURES: Buyer ____acknowledges *or* ____ does not acknowledge receipt of above Riders.

COMMISSION TO BROKER: The Seller hereby recognizes _____ as the Broker in this transaction, and agrees to pay as commission _____% of the gross sales price, or the sum of _____ Dollars ($_____) or one-half of the deposit in case same is forfeited by the Buyer through failure to perform, as compensation for services rendered, provided same does not exceed the full amount of the commission.

DEPOSIT RECEIPT

Deposit received by: (Print) _____ (Signature) _____

The above individual received the amount specified in Paragraph 2(a) on _____, _____.

TIME FOR ACCEPTANCE OF OFFER

Buyer offers to purchase the Property on the above terms and conditions. Unless this contract is accepted by the Seller and a copy delivered to the Buyer no later than _____ ____A.M. ____P.M. on _____, _____, this contract

continued . . .

may be revoked at Buyer's option, and Buyer's deposit refunded subject to clearance of funds.

BUYER

Date: _____ Buyer: _____ Tax ID No. _____

Date: _____ Buyer: _____ Tax ID No. _____

Phone: _____ Address: _____

Fax: _____

SELLER

Date: _____ Seller: _____ Tax ID No. _____

Date: _____ Seller: _____ Tax ID No. _____

Phone: _____ Address: _____

Fax: _____

Company Name and address
(If applicable)

No representation as to the legal validity or adequacy of any provision of this form is made. If you have questions, seek legal counsel prior to executing any contract.

Buyer (___) (___) and Seller (___) (___) acknowledge receipt of a copy of this page, which is page 4 of 4 pages.

CHAPTER 6

WHAT YOU NEED TO KNOW ABOUT HOME INSPECTIONS

In the previous chapter we discussed contracts and contract clauses. One of the most critical portions of a contract, the one that can easily make or break your contract, is the "inspection, repairs and maintenance" clause. Although most contracts will be pre-printed with 1% or 2% of the purchase price allowance for repairs, you are not obligated to accept that. It can be changed to 1/2 of 1%, or a flat dollar amount, or any amount you desire. You can believe that a buyer who knows you will pay up to $10,000 for repairs will find at least $10,000 worth of repairs that need to be done.

Generally, home inspectors are licensed by and qualified by the state to conduct inspections of homes and determine what, if anything, needs repairing or replacing. What will they inspect? Here is a partial list:

- *The roof*—For leaks, damage or age problems

- *Termites*—Signs of termites in the building or foundation, and termite damage

- *Dry rot*—Most homes experience dry rot where wood is exposed to the outside elements

- *Appliances*—That they are all in working order

- *Heating and air conditioning systems*—To insure that they are working properly and not old enough to be ready to break down

- *Plumbing*—Signs of leaks, dripping faucets, partially clogged sewer lines, toilet tank leaks or continual running, etc. Water heaters are also inspected.

- *Electrical*—Is it up to code or are there violations? Are all electric light switches and wall sockets working?

- *Exterior condition of home*—Settling cracks, paint peeling etc. Some hairline cracks are common as a home settles, but are there any signs of structural damage?

- *Interior condition of home*—Signs of leaks in walls or ceilings, general condition

- *Windows and doors*—Are they in good condition and sealed from the elements?

- *Insulation*—Is there adequate, up-to-code insulation in the attic to meet the building code requirements?

TAKING THE HOME INSPECTION IN STRIDE

There are other areas a good inspector will cover. (See the complete sample inspection report in Chapter 17.) The final result will be a multi-page report outlining all deficiencies the inspector found and an estimate of repair cost. Don't be surprised to see a whole list of things that are wrong with your home. Most of them will be minor, such as a dripping water faucet, and can easily be repaired. Big items, such as roof damage or termites, will require more outlay of cash to correct. This is where your repair limit comes into effect. If the estimated cost far exceeds what you agreed to allow, you and the buyer will have to discuss it and try to come to some agreement.

One more point about home inspectors. They are paid by the buyer to check out every detail in a home and report even the slightest problem or possible problem. This is why the list of items in need of repair will usually be a long one. The inspector is getting paid to find something wrong; if there isn't a list, the buyer will wonder if the wrong inspector was hired. Again, review the items listed. Correcting most of them is easy. After that, there is always negotiation with the buyer to help resolve the problems so a closing will take place as planned.

NEW AREAS FOR INSPECTIONS

In recent years, the government has mandated some new inspections:

- *Radon Gas:* Radon gas is an odorless and colorless gas that is sometimes found in the earth's rock and soil. Areas that are known to have a radon gas risk may require an inspection to see if the gas has infiltrated the house. The test is a simple canister placed in the home for several hours and then taken to a lab for analysis.

- *Lead-Based Paint:* We have known for some time that lead-based paint can be a health hazard if ingested. That usually occurs with small children who "teeth" on crib rails, windowsills, etc., that were painted with a lead-based paint. It has been banned for several years, but older homes may still have it in wooden portions of the home. Paint samples are scraped from the suspected areas for analysis.

- *Asbestos:* Homes built in the early 1970s and before often had asbestos tile floors and asbestos ceiling tiles. This substance, again, has been proven to pose a health risk and must be removed from the home. Quite often, in the case of asbestos ceiling tiles, it is possible to "encapsulate" the asbestos by applying paint over the surface.

WHAT SHOULD THE SELLER DISCLOSE?

After living in the home for a number of years, you are aware of the "faults" you may have discovered during the years. They can be in two major areas:

1. Defects in the home: You know that there is a problem with the home settling. The question is, is it noticeable to a potential buyer? Normal settling cracks in the exterior walls are common. They often occur within the first year or so after the home is built. In most

cases they are visible on the outside walls and are not serious. If, however, you have been told there is a major problem under the foundation that cannot easily or inexpensively be cured, this fact must be brought to a buyer's attention. This is especially true if the defect cannot be easily seen.

2. Disclosures that do not involve the home itself. Suppose you know that the State Highway Commission is planning to build a major Interstate highway that will just skirt the back edge of your property. This factor, as much as you don't want to mention it to a buyer, should be disclosed. As a practical matter, it is better to convey the truth now than to be sued in the future when the buyer realizes you withheld information that would have influenced the decision to buy.

This disclosure can take on several different areas of consideration. For example, if someone died a violent death in the home, you may have to disclose that fact. If, however, they died from AIDS, you cannot, by Federal law, disclose that fact.

SHOULD THE SELLER HAVE A HOME INSPECTION?

So far we have discussed how the buyer will require, and should require, a home inspection as a contingency in the contract. The purpose, of course, is to insure that there are no major problems with a home that must be addressed prior to closing or that could alter the market value of the home.

What we need to discuss here is the suggestion that a seller may want at least a limited home inspection prior to putting a home on the market. Why? To avoid any (expensive) surprises when the buyer has an inspection made. It does not have to be a full-blown inspection of every electrical outlet in the house, every water faucet, etc. But you want to check the "big ticket" items such as roof, termites, heating/air conditioning system, etc. If, for example, the roof is in poor condition or the home has termites, it is wise to recognize that fact before the buyer's inspector discovers it. This gives you the opportunity to correct the situation right away and eliminates one more problem the buyer can use to negotiate a lower price. You gain some advantages here. Let's assume you have an inspection and termites are found in the home.

1. You can probably correct the situation before the buyer's inspection. Your cost will usually be less than what the buyer would want to collect for the same treatment.

2. You can show the buyer that you have had the home inspected for termites or the roof repaired and that you have a warranty on it.

3. Even if you do not sell the home, you still need to have these problems corrected. If you ignore them, they will become even bigger problems later.

FIXING THE PROBLEMS

If problems are found by the buyer's inspection team and need to be corrected, make sure you get at least two bids for the work that needs to be done. Don't expect the buyer's brother-in-law to give you a fair estimate. There could even be situations where you both have an inspection made and the price to repair the damage differs widely. It may be necessary to have a third estimate made, by an independent contractor, agreed to by both you and the buyer.

CHAPTER 7

WHAT TO DO
IF YOUR HOME
WON'T SELL

You've done everything right. You've fixed up your home, advertised it, held Open Houses, priced it at fair market value, and it still doesn't sell. You've had a few "nibbles" but no offers to purchase. What do you do now?

First of all, check the current market conditions. Are other, comparable homes near you selling? If not, it may be a down market. If people just aren't buying, you may have to change tactics or plan on holding on until the market turns around again. Keep in mind, however, that even in a slow market, the price and condition of your home are vital to making a sale.

- *Tactic Number 1.* Take another look at the price you are asking. Are you sure the home is priced at a fair market value? If other homes in the area are selling, how are they priced compared to yours? Your home may really be worth your $175,000 asking price, but if only $125,000 homes are selling, you may have to hold out for better market conditions in order to obtain your price. If you really need to sell and will admit that you have your home overpriced, now is the time to lower it to a more realistic level.

- *Tactic Number 2.* Perhaps you started your marketing effort when you were in a seller's market. Now it's different. Now you need to pull out all of the stops in your marketing efforts. That includes advertising, Open Houses and any other marketing technique you can think of. If your ads are not getting responses, change them.

Appeal to a different market segment. Instead of concentrating on the beauty of the home, advertise how close it is to schools, or how great a family home it is. Try different newspapers, if they are available in your area. Advertise on different days of the week. Generally weekends draw the most interest.

- *Tactic Number 3.* If it becomes obvious that nothing is working and you have re-examined your marketing plan for mistakes you may have made or possible tactics you may have overlooked, quit spending money on advertising for awhile. Wait until the market improves.

- *Tactic Number 4.* Offer potential buyers some concessions or favorable terms. If you can carry a mortgage, or a small short-term second mortgage, you can attract a larger market of potential buyers. This will appeal to someone who cannot qualify for a large mortgage or who has limited cash available for a down payment.

Important Point: If you are willing to carry a mortgage, especially a second mortgage, you need to use caution and carefully screen your buyer. Unless you need your money out of the property immediately, you may want to consider selling your home on a lease/purchase agreement, where a potential buyer leases your home for a certain period of time. A portion of each rent payment is credited toward a down payment. Once there is sufficient equity built up by the tenant, title is transfered over. This does two things. It gives you time to be certain the tenant (buyer) can meet financial obligations of monthly payments, and it gives you the added security of knowing that the buyer has a reasonable amount of equity in the property before being given title. Financing techniques and lease/purchase agreements are discussed in Chapter 15.

TRYING TO SELL IN A SLOW MARKET

We mentioned earlier that you want to market your home during a Seller's market when homes are scarce. Unfortunately you may not be able to time the market that closely. You may have to sell because of a transfer to another area by your company or because of financial situations. The market could also change a short time after you start marketing your home.

Important Point: If you are being transferred by your company, find out if it has a "home purchase" plan for employees it transfers. Although your company may not pay top dollar, many will pay what they consider fair market value for your home, and the urgency of trying to sell will have been removed from your shoulders.

Assuming you have some control over the sale of your home, you have several choices.

The best alternative, of course, is to hold off selling your home until the market improves. If you need to sell in a down market, be prepared to accept less than if the home was being offered in a "hot" market. You need to use your judgment by comparing what it has been worth having the home during the time you lived there compared with the amount you will need to reduce the selling price to have it sold.

You need to determine the benefits you received while living in your present home. If you have lived in the home for a few years, it will have appreciated. It may have appreciated less than you had hoped, but it should still be worth more than you paid. You also need to weigh what it may cost you to wait until the market improves. If you are trying to reduce your living expenses, and must keep paying on the present home for an additional six months, how will that cost compare with the savings you will realize by selling quickly at a lower price? Don't forget to add in the cost of higher utility bills, taxes, insurance, etc. If you plan on saving $1,000 a month in your new home, if you wait six months for a market turnaround, it just cost you $6,000.

There may be another motivating factor for a quick sale, even in a down market. Assuming money is not the primary reason, you just want out. Perhaps you've found another home that is your dream house. If you don't tie it up quickly, you will probably lose it. It may pay you to price your home for a quick sale. If you can afford to do so, you may want to consider renting your present home for six months or a year. Ideally, you can rent it for enough to cover your mortgage, tax and insurance costs.

GETTING YOUR HOME SOLD WHEN IT'S A FINANCIAL NECESSITY

Your home has been on the market for some time and you are still unable to find a buyer. You need to get out from under the expense of home ownership without hurting your credit standing. What do you do? There is a "last ditch" method of getting out from under your home expense. There are real estate brokers and independent companies who will buy your home if you cannot sell it and need to get out of it.

Here is how most of them work. First of all, you need to understand that appraisals on a property are usually well below its fair market value. (When we discuss "Working with Appraisers," you'll learn how appraisers estimate the value of a home.) Here is another fact about appraisals. If you are having your home appraised for a mortgage, the lender will usually have its own appraiser do the work. Since the appraiser works for the lender, and the lender is basing the loan value of the property on the appraiser's estimate of value, you can be sure that that estimate will, in most cases, be very conservative. The appraiser does not want the lender to come back later and ask why a home on which it loaned $120,000 is really only worth $110,000.

With that background thought in mind, here is what to expect if someone who will buy your home approaches you. You already know that the appraised value will probably be less than what the fair market value should be. Furthermore, the potential buyer/investor of your home will generally offer you less than the appraised value.

Example: A home that, in a normal market, should sell for $125,000 has an appraised value of $110,000. The home buyer may offer to "take it off your hands" for $95,000. He or she can then hold it until the market turns around and make a $30,000 profit before closing costs. If the buyer happens to be a real estate broker, he or she will greatly reduce those closing costs by the amount of the commission.

CHAPTER 8

ALL ABOUT THE CLOSING

This is the day you have been waiting for. You managed to sell your home yourself. You followed the suggestions in this book, were able to realize a profit, and save the cost of a real estate fee. Now it's time to attend the closing. We will discuss what it will cost, what to take with you, and then what to expect when you attend.

ESTIMATING YOUR CLOSING COSTS

As you know, you will be subject to some closing costs when you sell your home. Listed on page 68 is a simple closing statement with the majority of items you may find on your closing statement. Each line has been numbered for reference. Below the form is a brief description of each charge, what it is and how much it could run.

SELLER CLOSING STATEMENT
ESTIMATED COSTS

Item	Charge Seller	Credit Seller
1. Sales Price		_____
2. Escrow Account Balance		_____
3. Existing 1st Mortgage Payoff	_____	
4. Existing 2nd Mortgage Payoff	_____	
5. Real Estate Taxes to Closing Date	_____	
6. Settlement Fees (Attorney)	_____	
7. Abstract or Title Insurance	_____	
8. Document Preparation Fee	_____	
9. Recording Fee (if applicable)	_____	
10. Inspection Fees (if applicable)	_____	
11. Other _____	_____	
12. Total Charges and Credits	_____	_____
13. Net Proceeds to Seller		_____

(Credits—Charges)

NOTE: The above items are for this example only. A formal closing statement will be prepared by the closing agent and given to you, the seller, prior to closing. It may contain items not found on this list.

Also, some of the charges shown may not be applicable in a given area. Others may be added that are not included here. Check with your attorney or closing agent.

In most areas you can expect seller closing costs to average about 1% or 2%. As we review each item, you'll see how a typical closing statement is prepared.

1. *Sales Price:* This is the final negotiated price that you and the buyer agreed to.

2. *Escrow Account Balance:* If you have a mortgage on the property, the lender no doubt maintains an escrow account to cover real estate taxes and insurance. You will notice this charge on your monthly mortgage payment invoice. By the time the annual tax and insurance bills come in, there should be enough money in the escrow account to cover both. Generally, tax bills will be mailed prior to the end of the year. You may be entitled to a discount if you pay the bill in November. Your lender will want enough money in the escrow account to pay the bill when it arrives in November to take advantage of the discount. This means, when you bought your home, you probably were charged for November and December's taxes as part of your closing costs. Now, when you sell, you are entitled to any money left in the escrow account minus the amount you owe for the portion of the year you owned your home. That includes your share of real estate taxes and insurance. Item Number 2 generally shows the total amount in the escrow account. Adjustments to that amount are made below.

3. *Existing 1st Mortgage Payoff:* You will be charged (debited) for the remaining balance due on the mortgage as of the day of closing.

4. *Existing 2nd Mortgage Payoff:* If there is a second mortgage on the property, you will also be debited for the remaining balance on that mortgage as of the day of closing.

5. *Real Estate Taxes Due at Closing:* In Number 2, you received credit for the amount left in the escrow account. Item Number 5 charges you for the portion of real estate taxes you owe for the year.

6. *Settlement Fees (Attorney):* If you employ an attorney to handle the closing for you, the appropriate fee is listed here.

7. *Abstract or Title Insurance:* Some states have "Abstracts of Title." They are written and recorded histories of each change of title from the time it was first acquired by the United States. If your state has Abstracts, the seller is usually responsible to pay to have the Abstract brought current.

   Title insurance insures the property against any cloud or any title problem that may arise prior to your buying a property. It's an insurance policy. Your title policy also protects you from any problem that may arise at any time after you sell the property for something that is being questioned during your time of ownership. For example, a question may arise, during a future title search, that an improper signature was on the deed. You signed the deed Rob Hunter and it should have been Robert G. Hunter. Even though you no longer own the property, your title policy protects you from any loss and will resolve the problem for you. Title insurance, as you might realize, is a very important policy to buy, even though it may be optional in your state.

   As a seller, if Abstracts are not in effect, you will probably be expected to pay for the cost of a title insurance policy for the buyer. Other than the real estate fee, this is often the single most expensive charge to a seller. It is based on the selling price of the property, and is a one-time charge.

8. *Document Preparation Fee:* This is the charge for the preparation of the paperwork necessary to transfer title to your property. It includes

the preparation of the deed, a list of personal property being included in the sale, and an affidavit of no liens (which states that, "to the best of your knowledge there are no outstanding debts on the property except those of record" such as the mortgage). If you hire an attorney to handle the closing, it will be included in the legal fees.

9. *Recording Fees (If applicable):* Generally it is the buyer's responsibility to pay to have the deed recorded in the county courthouse. (It is in a buyer's best interest to do so.) If you are carrying a mortgage, however, you will want to have it recorded as well. That will be at your expense.

10. *Inspection Fees (If applicable):* If you agreed to pay for the home inspection, it will be entered here.

11. *Other:* This will include items that are not on the list above. Perhaps you agreed to pay for repairs that were not completed. That amount due the buyer will be entered here assuming it was a payout figure to the buyer and he or she will be taking care of the repairs.

    NOTE: If there are repairs that have not been completed, it is general practice to have the closing company or attorney hold the agreed-upon funds in escrow until the repairs are completed. Any remaining balance, after the work is completed and paid for, is returned to the seller.

12. *Total Charges and Credits:* Total each column of figures and enter them here.

13. *Net Proceeds to Seller:* Subtract the total charges from the credits. The remaining balance is the amount due to you at closing.

    NOTE: Your closing agent should give you a copy of the closing statement a day or two prior to closing.

If all goes well, your next task is to attend the closing on the sale. We'll discuss that next.

But first, we need to discuss one more important factor.

CLOSING WITHOUT MONEY

Unless you are quite well off, you will need the funds from the home you are selling in order to close on your new one. It's like the "chicken or the egg" dilemma. If you wait until the closing on your home for the money you need, you will have no place to live until you can close on your new home because it is customary to give occupancy on the day of closing.

Conversely, how can you close on your new home before you receive the funds from the one you are selling? Although we suggested a few ways in another part of this book, the best solution may be a "bridge loan."

Using a Bridge Loan

In simple terms, a bridge loan is a "temporary" loan that you obtain from your lender until the permanent one can be put in place. Once the primary mortgage is in place, the bridge loan is paid off and closed out.

Although it may not always be a necessity, it helps to have a firm contract on the sale of your home before approaching a lender. You can show that the funds you need to pay off the bridge loan will be forthcoming. You may not need this if you have an excellent credit rating since some lenders will establish the loan for you based on that credit, your assets, etc.

There is usually a quid pro quo that really is not bad. If you secure a bridge loan from a lender, you should, or may be expected to, get the permanent loan from that lender. It's only fair. In the "Buyer" section of this book we discuss the importance of getting pre-qualified for a mortgage before you look for a home. You have now become the buyer and should follow that same advice. You gain three major advantages by doing so.

1. You know how much home you are qualified to buy, before you fall in love with one that is way beyond your means.

2. You have considerably more bargaining power with sellers if they know you already have pre-qualified for a mortgage and can afford to buy their home. Let's look at this for a moment from a seller's point of view. The biggest problem you face as a seller is in not knowing if

a suspect, who looks at your home, can really qualify to buy it. Notice I said "suspect" and not "prospect" or "buyer." When you first have a looker at your home, you never know if that person is serious about buying your home and can qualify to do so, or if this is just someone with nothing better to do than look at homes that are for sale, a suspect. If, however, someone comes in who is already pre-qualified with a lender for a home in your price range, you have a "live one."

You also know, as a seller, that you have a "live one" if that looker is closing on a present home in three weeks or has been transferred to your area by the employing company and will be moving into town next month. You don't want to lose that buyer. You need to quickly find a way of giving the buyer occupancy of your home whenever it is needed. This will give you the ammunition you need for step three.

3. Now as a buyer, you open the door with that lender for a possible bridge loan. The lender already knows you are qualified to buy a specific home and, armed with a contract on the sale of your home, you can show the lender that you are just waiting to close on yours in order to buy the new one. Since banks are in the business of loaning money, the loan officer will probably see a long-term, secured mortgage on the books, if he or she helps you with the financing until the new mortgage can be put into place.

Important Point: While waiting for a closing on your home, you will be making two mortgage payments. You will owe your present mortgage payment plus the payment on the bridge loan. Be certain you can afford it.

Once you have a bridge loan, you can finance the gap between closing on your present home and closing on the new one. You can also breathe more easily knowing you'll have a place to live on the day of closing of your present home.

Tax Consequences on Your Profit

Important Point: The information in this section is current as of the publication date of this book. Tax laws are continually changing. You are advised to use this section only as a guide. Consult with your tax counsel to determine the tax consequences on the sale of your home.

Great! You sold your home and made a nice profit. Unfortunately, Uncle Sam may want to share it. I say "may want to share" because our new, "friendlier" IRS has given homeowners some big tax breaks on the profit they make when they sell their homes. You must, however, meet certain guidelines.

As the law currently reads, here is what the IRS allows you to do:

1. You must qualify under home ownership and use conditions as follows:

   During the five-year period prior to selling, the home must have been owned and used by the taxpayer as the principal residence for periods totaling two years or more.

   That two-year minimum does not have to be continuous. (You may have lived in the home for a year, rented it out for a couple of years, and then moved in for another year or longer.)

2. A seller of any age can qualify for a $250,000 exclusion of taxation of the profit. This rule has become more generous. First of all, there is no longer an age 55 or older limitation on the exclusion allowance: Any age taxpayer qualifies for the tax break. Secondly, the amount of the exclusion has been increased from $125,000 to $250,000.

3. If you are filing a joint tax report, the exclusion is increased to $500,000.

   (**NOTE:** There are some additional rules involved. Talk to your tax counsel for the most recent details.)

4. If the home is sold because of change in employment, health reasons or due to some other unforeseen circumstances, some or all of the gain from a home sale may be excluded even if the taxpayer does not meet the above tests.

5. There are other factors that are part of the tests for tax exemption which are not covered in this section. Again, you are advised to seek

tax counsel when you sell to insure that you meet the requirements for tax breaks on your profit.

6. You also need to check with your state laws. Some states also tax profit on the sale of a home.

Let's look at how your profit on the sale is calculated. Here is the simple formula based on your meeting the above requirements.

Selling Price: _____

Less: Purchase Price
(What you paid for it) _____

Less: Cost of Purchase:

    Attorney Fees _____

    Real Estate Commissions _____

    Title Insurance _____

    Recording Fees _____

    Advertising Expense _____

    Loan Origination Costs _____
    (when you bought)

    Other Purchase Expenses _____

    Less: Capital Improve-
    ments* (new roof,
    appliances, etc.) _____

Total Costs: _____

Adjusted Cost Basis: _____

Capital Gain on Sale: _____

*Capital Improvements do NOT include repair and maintenance items, such as painting, fixing a leaking water faucet or planting new shrubs.

Example:

Selling Price of Home:			$200,000
Less Purchase Price:		$100,000	
Less: Costs: Title Insurance	$ 850.00		
Real Estate Fees	6,000.00		
Other Costs	450.00		
Total Costs:		$ 7,300.00	
Less: Capital Improvements:			
New Roof	$ 4,000.00		
New Refrigerator	1,000.00		
Total Capital Improvements:		$ 5,000.00	
Adjusted Cost Basis:			$112,300
Profit on Sale:			$ 87,700

Your "taxable" profit is $87,700, which, as you now know, will probably not be taxable at all.

See, the IRS has gotten friendlier!

One final point: Taxable or not, the sale must be reported to the IRS. In fact, your closing agent (attorney or title company) will file the required forms to the IRS after the closing takes place.

WHAT TO BRING TO THE CLOSING

Before you close, notify your mortgagee immediately in writing that your house has been sold and what the status of the mortgage will be (paid off at closing or assumption by buyer).

Gather your receipted bills for taxes, water, condo/homeowners association dues/fees.

Notify utilities when to make a final reading on your meters and/or change over services.

Use the Pre-Closing Checklist on page 84.

Prepare a list of all service people you either have under contract or have used. If the buyer is taking over your service contracts (or is obligated to retain them until the next renewal date), you need to provide all of the materials and documents relating to the contracts. You will find a useful Seller Checklist on page 85.

What services may be under a contract? Pest control, air conditioning and heating or lawn service. Many of these services are on a month-to-month basis, so contract obligations do not concern the buyer. Another common service contract that you may have is the home maintenance contract which provides for servicing appliances and heating/air conditioning systems, etc.

Other non-contract services include the people you use for general repairs and maintenance, swimming pool maintenance, etc. You want to furnish your buyer with a list of names, addresses and phone numbers of each of these services. The new owner may not want to use them, but at least will know who has been doing these things for you. It may be convenient to continue using them until there is time to employ someone else.

What else do you need to take to closing?

- Keys to your home
- Garage door openers
- Blueprints, surveys, and any other documentation on the home that you may have
- Any information that may be helpful to the buyer

It is also helpful to furnish the buyer with a list of the various utility companies and their phone numbers. When someone is new to the area, it is often difficult to know who to call for these services. They include:

- Water and sewer service
- Electric

- Telephone
- Cable TV
- Trash removal

Some sellers even furnish the buyer with a list of convenient numbers for such things as:

- Voter registration and where to vote
- Local council representatives
- Non-emergency numbers for local police and fire departments and nearest hospital
- Any other services that may be needed

When you first moved into your home, chances are you had to research all of these services yourself. Being new to the area made it difficult. It's a helpful, much appreciated courtesy to give your buyers this information. (Use the Critical Information for the Buyer form on page 86.)

WHAT HAPPENS AT THE CLOSING

You will be signing a stack of documents. These will include the following:

- Deed to your home
- Bill of sale for any personal property being conveyed
- Closing statement
- No lien affidavit—This document may be signed by both parties and indicates that there are no outstanding bills or encumbrances on the property, other than those agreed to by both parties.
- Mortgage documents, if you are carrying a mortgage

You will receive a check for the proceeds of the sale. It should correspond to the amount shown on your closing statement. That statement is the one that you should have received a day or two before the closing.

If you did receive such a statement a day or two before the closing, or the closing was delayed a day or two, the amount of the final closing statement, and therefore the check amount, may be different from what you were expecting. If you have any questions, be sure to ask them; request details on why the amount is different.

A delay in closing can affect several different things:

- The amount of interest you owe on the mortgage for the period of time between the originally scheduled closing date and the actual date must be paid.

- Your portion of real estate taxes for that additional day or two must be paid.

- There could be a mistake in the figures, Yes, that can happen and often does.

You will need confirmation that all of the agreed-upon repairs have been made and paid for. If some repairs have yet to be made, it is generally acceptable to have the necessary funds escrowed to cover the cost of these repairs. Any excess funds will be returned to the seller. The escrow or closing agent or attorney will hold the funds.

Be certain to verify that the amount on the check you receive is correct, according to the current closing statement. Your closing agent or attorney should cover each item with you in order to insure you know how the final dollar amount was reached.

At first, the paperwork you will face will seem overwhelming. However, if you have traded your old car in for a new one, you have waded through more paperwork in that transaction than in buying or selling a house.

Expect minor glitches or disagreements. Rarely does a closing take place without a hitch. Generally, it can be worked out with few problems. More on this subject later.

After all of the paperwork has been executed and all of the keys and documents have been disbursed, you can take great satisfaction in knowing that you did it on your own and saved several thousands of dollars.

HANDLING UNEXPECTED PROBLEMS

It is important to remember that most closings take place without any problems. Even if there is a problem, it can generally be worked out at the closing table.

So, breathe a little easier. The purpose of this discussion is merely to point out some of the typical problems or "glitches" that can crop up at the closing. You may never experience one, but it does not hurt to know what can happen and how to solve the problem if it occurs.

Here is a list of the most common problems that seem to wait until closing to show up.

TITLE PROBLEMS

This may include a break in the title transfer chain long before you purchased the property. It was not caught when you bought the home. To further complicate this situation, the past owner in question has now died and the title company must trace back to see who now can execute a "Quitclaim Deed" to relinquish any interest in the property. (That's why you have title insurance.) To complicate the matters even more, there are now four children who are heirs to the estate of that individual and they are scattered all over the country; in fact one is in Europe. They all have to sign the quitclaim deed. It can be worked out; the only problem is, it might take time.

Important Point: Unless the problem turns out to be insurmountable, you can generally proceed with the closing anyway. Title may not be transferred until any defect is cured. All the documents (and your cash proceeds) will be held by the Title Company or attorney until the problem is resolved. At least you won't have to sit through another closing. Only in rare exceptions will it take a long period of time to solve most title problems.

CLOSING COSTS

The estimated closing costs are different from what you thought they would be. The buyer may find that the assumable mortgage balance is much lower than originally thought. This means additional cash is needed to close. You might discover that you must pay off a lien against the property or some other expense is involved that was not caught before closing.

Important Point: Anyone with just cause (sometimes without just cause) can file a lien against your property. It probably will never be noticed until you are ready to sell. Chances are you won't even remember what the reason for the lien is or who might have filed it. It does not matter. One way or another, it has to be resolved and that's what your attorney gets paid to do.

TERMITE TROUBLE

Your contract calls for a termite inspection. It has been said that there are two types of homes, those that have termites and those that will have termites. Generally they can be treated with little problem. In extreme circumstances, the home may have to be "tented" and fumigated, and any damage repaired. This problem should have been caught by the home inspection people long before closing. By the day of closing, the damage should have been assessed and repaired. In the event a termite problem is discovered and is not corrected by the day of closing, the necessary funds to correct the problem can be escrowed and the closing can take place as planned.

ENCROACHMENTS

When a new survey is completed for the mortgage lender, it is discovered that a storage shed, fence or some other type of structure is sitting over the property line on the neighbor's land. This will have to be corrected before a title policy can be written for the buyer.

FINAL FIGURES AND CHARGES

You get to the closing and discover that the settlement figures differ from the figures you were given prior to closing. This is where Murphy's Law comes into effect. It does not seem to matter if you are the buyer or seller, the error will not be in your favor. If you owe the additional funds, they will be deducted from your proceeds. If the buyer came to the closing with a check that does not include the revised added amount, the closing agent will generally accept a personal check for the difference.

PRE-CLOSING INSPECTION PROBLEM

Your buyer has a right to walk through your house the day before or the day of closing to confirm that the condition is the same as it was when the contract was executed. The buyer will also verify that the items that were supposed to be left are still there. If any repairs were to be done, they should also have been completed by the time this "walkthrough" is made.

If certain agreed-to repairs are not completed by the closing date, it is usually possible to withhold (or escrow) the funds required to make them. This will allow the closing to proceed as scheduled.

MY HOME WON'T BE READY FOR TWO WEEKS

You are about ready to have a closing on the sale of your home. Everything is running smoothly . . . except for one minor problem. The home you are buying will not be ready to move into for another two weeks after the closing on your present home. The normal procedure is to give occupancy on the day of closing of title, so you have a problem. It's like the "chicken or the egg" dilemma. What comes first, closing of title on your present home or on your new one that won't be ready for two weeks? Let's look at the alternatives:

Possible Solution 1

You can delay the closing on your present home until your new one is ready. The problem here is that your buyers probably won't like the idea. This is especially true if they have their moving van sitting in front of your home, ready to move in on the original scheduled day of closing. If, however, they can be a little flexible on the day they intend to move in, you may have a chance at delaying the closing. The possible problem is that delaying the closing can be risky. Most home buyers get the jitters when they reach the closing table. They are about to commit to a huge sum of money and a large, long-term mortgage. If they have to think about it for another week or two, they really get nervous. They may even want to find a way out of the contract. After all, you are no doubt in breach of contract if you do not close on or near the scheduled closing date spelled out in the contract. An astute buyer, who panics at the thought of buying your home, can probably use that "closing shall be on or about June 15th" as an out.

Possible Solution 2

Leave the actual date of closing on your contract open (to negotiation) provided both parties agree to this arrangement. There must be some type of agreed-upon time limit, but there are occasions when the buyer may like some additional time to be certain a closing takes place on his or her home so the funds are available to close on yours.

Possible Solution 3

If the buyer is flexible on a move-in date, you may be able to work out an agreement to stay on in your home for those two weeks after the closing.

> **CAUTION:** There are potential problems in doing this. First of all, some type of compensation should be made to the buyer for allowing you to "rent his or her home" for that two-week period. Second, you run the risk of having something go wrong during that period, either because of your occupancy or because the buyer has second thoughts about the transaction.

Always have some type of written agreement, even if it is an informal document, outlining the terms of the "rental period" and the obligations on both parties. This solution, at least, allows the closing to take place on your present home. You will have your funds in hand for your new home.

Possible Solution 4

Let the closing take place as planned and you rent a motel for that two-week period. What about your furniture? Moving companies will store it for you, for a fee. If the waiting period is a short one, they may even leave it stored in the moving van until it is delivered to your new home. This is not a cost-free solution, but it does insure that the closing on your home takes place as scheduled. If you are relying on the funds from that sale to close on your new home, you don't want to do anything to jeopardize that closing.

If you need the funds from your present home in order to close on your second one, consider taking out a bridge loan.

Pre-Closing Checklist

____ Notify the mortgagee. Date: _____

____ Notify utilities when to make a final reading on your meters and/or change over services.

Water Department: Final reading date: _____

Power and Light: Final reading date: _____

Telephone Company: Date for change of service: _____

____ Notify cable television company.

____ Cancel any regular deliveries, i.e., newspaper.

____ Notify garbage/trash removal company.

____ Send change-of-address cards.

____ Transfer homeowner's insurance policy *after closing.*

____ Put all appliance/household equipment information in a kitchen cabinet drawer.

____ Remove all personal belongings from home.

____ Have home broom-swept clean.

____ Bring all keys, electric garage door openers to closing.

If home is vacant:

____ Notify police.

____ Arrange for lawn and pool care until day of closing.

____ Have a neighbor keep an eye on the house.

Seller Checklist: What to Take to the Closing

Here is a list of the various things you should take to closing with you. They will be turned over to the buyer.

What to Take:

____ List of service people you use, with phone numbers

____ Lawn service

____ Repairs, general, appliances, etc.

____ Heating/Air conditioning

____ Exterminating

____ Keys to your home

____ Garage door openers

____ A list of all service contracts in effect

____ Blueprints, surveys and any other documentation on the house

____ Any information that may be helpful to the new buyer

What to Expect:

1. Signing a mile-high stack of documents (Deed, bill of sale for personal property, closing statement, etc.)

2. Minor glitches or disagreements (Rarely does a closing go without a hitch . . . but it can generally be worked out.)

3. A check for the proceeds of the sale

4. Confirmation that agreed repairs have been made and paid for. If not, monies will be escrowed to cover them.

5. A "No-lien" affidavit showing all bills have been paid except for those known and agreed to by both parties.

Critical Information for the Buyer

Welcome to the neighborhood! Here are important telephone numbers you will need.

Police/Fire:_____

Emergency Medical/Ambulance:_____

Water Company:_____

Electric/Gas/Oil Company:_____

Trash Removal:_____

Telephone Company:_____

Cable TV:_____

Landscaping Service:_____

Snow Removal:_____

Cleaning Service:_____

Town/City/Borough Hall:_____

Other:_____

Other:_____

Other:_____

Other:_____

PART TWO

BUYING YOUR HOME YOURSELF

Buying a home is probably the single most expensive purchase you will make in your lifetime. It is paramount that you take every precaution to avoid making a financial mistake. The first decision you need to make is whether to buy or rent. You need to consider several factors that may influence this decision.

How secure is your job and/or are you likely to get transferred in the near future?

What about your finances? Can you afford to buy a house or are you better off renting until you have additional cash to buy? The CD-ROM included with this book has a computer analysis program to help you make that decision.

Once you decide to buy a home, what kind do you want: a new home or a used one, a condominium or house? You also need to determine how much home you can afford; obviously there is no point in looking at homes you cannot afford to buy. You also do not want to get into financial trouble by overextending your budget. The CD-ROM will help you make this determination.

Then you need to find it. You'll find questions you should ask the seller and what to look for when visiting the home.

You will probably need a mortgage to buy your home, so you need to understand the "secrets" of getting the best financing. You'll learn about the various types of mortgages that are available and the pros and cons of each. You'll learn what to look out for when applying for a mortgage, how mortgages work, and where to find the best deal.

We'll show you how to prepare your offer to purchase. You want to offer the lowest price you can without being so insulting that the seller won't even talk to you, let alone consider your offer. You will also find out about certain contract clauses you should include in the offer to protect yourself. A sample contract is included.

We'll identify common mistakes buyers make and show you how to avoid making them.

Your offer has been accepted and you're ready to close on your house. You'll be shown what to expect at the closing; how much money you will need to close; how to understand your closing statement; other charges and prorations. You'll discover ways to save money on your closing costs.

Finally, you'll learn what you need to do immediately after the closing.

CHAPTER 9

MAKING THE
DECISION TO BUY

I know, you have your heart set on owning your own home. Almost everyone has that desire. Perhaps you already own a home and are thinking of making a change.

If you are a first-time home buyer, there are a few decisions you need to make before you jump into home ownership. The first one is, are you ready for this? That sounds like a dumb question to ask, since you are reading this book to learn how to do it. But you should first see where you are now in your life and financially, to make certain buying a home is the right move for you. Why would there be any doubt? You should consider these questions:

How secure are you in your present job? Is it logical to assume that you will be moving in the next year or so? Do you expect any of your circumstances to change enough in the next couple of years that will warrant a change of residence? If so, you may have difficulty selling the home you want to buy for enough to pay closing costs twice (once to buy it and once to sell it) and allow you to at least break even.

Now compare the cost of renting, with no other financial obligations except utilities, with the cost of home ownership. Home ownership costs include mortgage payments, taxes, insurance, repairs and maintenance, lawn care and more sizable utility bills. On top of that you have moving costs and startup costs in the new home.

Most people move into a home with two thoughts in mind. First, the idea of owning your own home is a nice feeling . . . the "American Dream." Second, they have the idea they will make money on their home. Not only will it appreciate, but they are paying off a mortgage each month, which is like money in the bank.

True, their home should appreciate, provided they do two things: First, buy in an appreciating neighborhood and, second, own the home long enough for appreciation to take effect. That is the reason to reconsider buying if you plan on living in the home for only a year or two. Chances are remote that it will appreciate much—or at all—during that short holding period. If it does, your profits will be eaten up by closing costs when you buy it and again when you sell. As far as paying down the mortgage, little if any will be paid off during two years of ownership. If you have a $100,000 mortgage on your home for 30 years at 8 percent interest, your monthly payments will be $733.76 a month. If you own that home for two years, your mortgage will be paid down to $98,260. You've made $17,610.24 in mortgage payments and you have only reduced the mortgage by $1,795. When we discuss mortgages in Chapter 15, you'll discover all the ins and outs of financing. The good news is that you will probably be able to deduct mortgage interest and real estate taxes from your income taxes.

That's enough about the negative side of buying a home. Now let's look at the positive side.

ADVANTAGES OF OWNING A HOME

As we mentioned, home ownership is the dream of most of us. Not only is there prestige in owning your own home, but also it has many side advantages. Obtaining credit is often easier if you are a homeowner rather than a renter.

You have some control over your living costs. Rents can increase annually but your mortgage is probably fixed for its duration. The only variables are taxes and insurance. Utility costs may increase, but they will also increase in the apartment you are renting. There is comfort in knowing you are in control of your own home. No one can ask you to leave, as long as you make mortgage payments and pay your other bills.

You don't have to be concerned about a landlord "bugging" you for all kinds of things, and you don't have to worry about noisy neighbors whom you can hear through the walls of the adjoining apartment.

You'll probably have considerably more space in your home than you did in an apartment.

You can redecorate any way you wish, even if it means tearing out an entire wall or replacing appliances.

If you like to work in the yard, you now have your own private space to plant and landscape any way you want. Chances are you'll have a garage, which you probably didn't have in your apartment.

Finally, when you sit back at night and look around, it's a good feeling to think, "This is mine!" even if the bank owns more than you do.

All right, you've made the decision to buy a home. Where do you start?

BUYING A NEW HOME OR AN EXISTING HOME

The first decision you may face is, "Should I buy a new home or a previously owned one?" There are advantages to each. You have to first determine what is available for sale when you want to buy, in the area you want and in your price range. This will eliminate most of the potential homes immediately. Here are some pros and cons about both new construction and older homes.

PROS AND CONS OF BUYING A NEW HOME

Pros: It's nice knowing you are the original owner of a home. Everything is brand new and under warranty. The only cleaning that may be needed is that of new construction that may not have been totally cleaned up. It's a lot better than cleaning up someone else's dirty oven or bathrooms.

The developer may be willing to work with you on financing and may even be willing to carry a small second mortgage if you need additional cash to close.

If the home is still being completed, you can generally select your own appliances, floor and wall coverings, countertops, etc. The builder will either give you an allowance for these items or adjust the price to cover any reduction (which probably will not be the case) or increase in cost based on what you select.

If you are handy, you may be able to do some of the finishing work yourself and get a discount from the developer.

Cons: You have to rely on the builder's integrity to insure everything is done correctly and completed. If the builder goes broke, which some do, you are left holding the bag with any problems you may have.

A new home will usually have some problems, such as settling cracks, poor fit on kitchen fixtures, wiring or plumbing problems, and some things that just will not work right. Although the developer will take care of these problems, they are still a nuisance you must put up with until they are resolved.

PROS AND CONS OF BUYING AN EXISTING HOME

Pros: You will generally have more square footage of space in a used home of comparable price. That is because it is competing with a new one, so the price, on a per-square-foot basis, will be less. This generally happens for two reasons. First, construction costs were less expensive when the home was built so the builder could give you more space for the same amount of money as new construction today. Second, since the home is "used," the seller realizes the price cannot be the same as for a new home.

Most of the problems you will find in a new home will have been resolved in an existing home. Any settling the home will do has already occurred. Problems with poor fitting of components have been eliminated.

If you want to locate in a well-established neighborhood, there may not be any vacant lots available. You will have to buy a used home.

Used homes have many amenities that you will have to add to a new construction, for example, window treatments. You may want to change the draperies, but all the rods are in place, saving you the expense and work of installation.

Neighbors are well established and you get a feeling of how nice (or bad) the neighborhood is before you buy.

Cons: Old homes are "old" homes. You can expect problems to arise that you should not have to face in a new one. Appliances, heating and air conditioning systems, electric systems and plumbing only last so long without needing upgrading. Roof leaks are a common problem. The older the home, the more problems you can expect.

Important Note: This is the reason you need a full inspection of a home as a contingency in your contract to purchase. Most of these problems will be caught and resolved prior to closing.

The bottom line is simple. Generally, you will buy the best of what is available, in the area you want to live in and can afford. There is one more decision you need to make. Should you consider a house, a town house or a condominium? Read on.

CHAPTER 10

SHOULD YOU BUY A HOUSE OR A CONDOMINIUM?

There are reasons for deciding to move into a house or a condominium. We have already discussed the various options available to you when you decide to move. We pointed out, briefly, that condominium living is ideal for "empty nesters" or couples who have grown children and are now alone. Once at retirement age, many condo owners like the ability to just lock the doors and leave without having to worry about their unit or security.

EXAMINE YOUR LIFESTYLE

Below you will find a list of lifestyles and how the usual choice between a house and a condo meets those needs.

YOUR LIFESTYLE	HOUSE	CONDO
Fairly young, still raising children	X	
Children grown and married		X
You enjoy working in the yard	X	
You hire for all of the yard work to be done		X
You like to travel, and do it often		X
You throw large parties	X	

You're "very" concerned about security		X
You like "space"	X	
You don't want anyone telling you what you can and cannot do	X	
You like to socialize and meet new people		X

As you can see, the choice becomes obvious depending on your lifestyle.

CONDOMINIUMS VS. COOPERATIVES

What is the difference between a condominium and a cooperative?

In a condominium, each apartment is individually owned and deeded to the owner. As a buyer, you own your own apartment/home within the overall complex. The common areas, such as hallways, clubhouse, pool, grounds, etc., are owned by all of the unit owners. Your monthly assessment for maintaining these facilities will be prorated over the number of units in the complex. That proportion will be redivided by assessing each unit owner in accordance with the size of the individual unit. Larger size units will be assessed more than the smaller ones.

Unlike condominiums, the owner in the cooperative complex does NOT have title to and a deed to the individual unit. Instead, the unit owner becomes a stockholder in the entire complex. A stock certificate is given to the co-op owner based again on the percentage of the overall complex that the unit represents. For example, if the complex is 100 units in size, the individual owner may own a one percent share in the overall complex. (This, again, will be adjusted by the size of the unit.)

So, which is better? Most buyers prefer the condominium type of ownership because they feel more secure in having an ownership deed to their apartment. Quite often, condos are easier to finance than co-ops. Although most prefer a condo, don't pass up a sound co-op if it has what you are looking for.

CAVEATS ABOUT BUYING A CONDOMINIUM

Unlike buying a house, buying an apartment in a condominium or co-operative means a change of lifestyle (which is the main reason for considering it). BUT, it also means carefully reviewing the "government" involved with the complex. Each condominium has an elected board of directors. They determine how the building will be run and how money will be spent in maintaining and upgrading the exterior of the buildings and the grounds and recreation facilities. You need to have a board pulling together for the betterment of the building. If it does not accomplish this, or directors are impossible to get along with, it is up to the majority of unit owners to replace them.

HOW RESTRICTIVE ARE THE CONDO BYLAWS?

Review the condo documents. (You will get a copy as an owner.) If you are still looking, ask if you might review the seller's copy. What will the board of directors allow and, more important, not allow? Here is a typical list of some things that may not be allowed. If you agree with everything on this list, this may be the right condo for you.

1. No Pets Allowed. (Some buildings allow pets but under a certain weight.)

2. Certain types of vehicles may not be allowed such as vans, pickup trucks, and vehicles with advertising on them, etc.

3. Children under a certain age may not be welcome, except for occasional visits.

4. The building may have a minimum age requirement, such as 55.

   NOTE: Discriminating against a potential unit owner because of age is against the law, but I know of at least one condo that maintains that it has always been a retiree-age building. It has won two lawsuits over people under the age of 55 who wanted to move into the building as unit owners.

5. You will probably have to conform to the window treatments that are allowed by the complex in order to keep the exterior appear-

ance uniform. This will also include exterior storm panels for the windows.

So, with all of these possible restrictions, why consider a condominium?

1. Carefree living . . . lock the door and leave.

2. Larger condos offer recreation facilities such as clubhouse, pool, tennis courts, spas, exercise rooms, planned activities, transportation to and from shopping, churches, doctor appointments, etc.

3. You have the opportunity to meet new people, make new friends. Living in the same building removes the barrier that faces a homeowner, where the next-door neighbor is isolated from you by lawns, fences and space.

4. Older residents like the security of the complex plus knowing someone is close when and if they need help.

LIVING IN A MAINTAINED COMMUNITY

A maintained community is one in which all of the units, condos or individual homes are under the management of a central association. A homeowners association is responsible for maintaining the entire complex. This includes grounds maintenance and building maintenance for all structures, even if they are single-family homes, detached or attached.

Attached homes are condominiums, cooperatives, town homes, villas, and single-family homes that all have common walls dividing the units. Detached homes are those that are free standing with no common walls between units.

WHAT YOU SHOULD KNOW ABOUT HOMEOWNERS ASSOCIATIONS

The homeowners association controls what is allowed and not allowed within the community. It is usually comprised of the homeowners and headed either by a member of the association or, in large communities, an outside manager. Their authority is governed by the bylaws of the association.

You must be very careful when buying a home or condo that is controlled by a condo association. Check it out carefully. Talk to some of the present owners (who are NOT on the association board). Ask them if they are having problems with the association. Chances are you have heard the term "Condo Commandos." It is used by some homeowners in maintained communities for the so-called "watchdog(s)" of the community. Some of these "watchdogs" have nothing better to do than keep an eye on your every move. This may sound like a harsh judgment on the association leaders, but unfortunately it is often deserved. In many cases the association has not given them the right to tell homeowners what they should or should not be doing . . . but they do it anyway. Horror stories are quite common. Most complaints are easy to resolve, but you want to know what to expect before you buy in that community.

Find Out About Monthly Association Fees

If you owned your own home, you would be faced with monthly charges for lawn care, exterior maintenance, trimming of shrubs, pool maintenance, etc. If you live in a maintained community, expect to pay a monthly homeowner fee to cover the cost of these services that will now be done through the homeowners association. This becomes important when you are comparing your monthly living expenses now with what they will be in a maintained community. You may be able to reduce your monthly mortgage payments by $100 a month, but you may be required to also pay a $150 a month in association fees. The same work may be done that would be done in your private home, but now you will be required to pay it on time every month. When you own your own home outside of a maintained community, you can let some maintenance expenses slide for a month or two if needed by delaying the repairs. You cannot do that in a maintained community. You also want to inquire if there are any planned increases in the monthly assessment.

Watch Out for Special Assessments

The homeowners association also decides what upgrading needs to be done and how much of the cost each homeowner must pay. It may be for new roofs, exterior painting or the remodeling of the clubhouse. In any event, you will be required to pay your proportionate share of those costs. The only break is if, for example, roofs need replacing on only one section of the community, only those owners who are affected will be assessed for the repairs.

Before you enter into a contract to buy a home or condo in a maintained community, check with the association to see if there are any pending or proposed assessments that could end up costing you thousands of dollars you had not planned on spending.

The defense of homeowners associations is that most of them do a good job of maintaining the appearance of their community; in fact, most maintained communities are better maintained than many residential neighborhoods and take the worry and work out of maintaining your personal residence. All lawns are evenly manicured and maintained. Homes are kept in like-new condition wherever possible. Your only concern is to determine if you can afford the cost of periodic repairs and upgrading when the association decides they are needed. This is a good reason to become involved in your community association and at least attend its meetings, especially when the agenda includes a discussion of upgrading or major renovations.

For the right kind of owners, condominiums are an excellent choice. Just be certain to get all of the facts before you buy into one.

For the purpose of this book, we will assume you have decided to buy a house.

CHAPTER 11

HOW TO FIND THE RIGHT HOUSE

Now that you have made the decision to buy a house, you will be faced with one main unanswered question: How do I find the right house for me? On the next several pages you will be led, step by step, through the process of locating your new home. You'll begin by filling in a computer analysis program that will help you determine how much house you are qualified to buy. You will then learn how to find the houses that fit your budget and what to look for when visiting them. You'll have a checklist to take with you, one for each house you visit, so you remember what questions to ask and what to look for. Filling in the form will help you remember what you saw when you get home later. You'll also learn how to tie up the home you want if you have to sell your present house first.

HOW MUCH HOUSE ARE YOU QUALIFIED TO BUY?

Before you begin your search for a home, the first thing you need to do is determine how much house you can afford to buy. There is no point in looking at $300,000 houses if you can only afford to buy one at $150,000. (Some people look at expensive homes as a hobby on weekends, with no intention of buying even if they could qualify. Real estate brokers "love" them.)

The CD-ROM tutorial you received with this book has a mortgage qualifier included. It allows you to plug in a couple of screens of information about your financial position and the program calculates how much house you can afford. There are four parts to the form which you need to fill in. They are:

PART I. YOUR ANNUAL INCOME:

Primary Income   _____

+ Spouse's Income   _____

+ Other Income*   _____

= Total Income

*Other income includes such things as: Child Support, Social Security Payments, Dividends, Royalties, etc.

PART II. MONTHLY EXPENSES:

Real Estate Taxes   _____

+ Credit Card Payments   _____

+ Car Payments   _____

+ Other Monthly Payments   _____

= Total Monthly Expenses   _____

NOTE: Monthly payments include installment purchases. Do not include utility bills, auto, gas, credit cards that are paid in full each month, etc.

Once these figures are filled in, the computer program, at the click of the "calculate" button, will figure your Gross Income for Loan Purposes and your Net Income for Loan Purposes.

More on this as we progress to the next section.

PART III. COST OF HOME YOU WANT TO BUY

Purchase Price   _____

– Your Down Payment   _____

= Mortgage Amount   _____

Mortgage Term (years)   _____

Interest Rate   _____

The program will calculate
  your monthly mortgage payment   _____

PART IV—ESTIMATED INCOME YOU WILL NEED TO QUALIFY FOR THIS MORTGAGE

Lenders generally use the two percentage figures below in qualifying you for a loan:

Gross Income × 28%   _____

Net Income × 36%   _____

Estimated Closing Cost (%)   _____

Estimated Closing Cost ($ amt.)   _____

+ Down Payment   _____

= Cash Needed for Closing   _____

Next you receive a "here's what it all means" list:

1. The mortgage amount you want to obtain is: _____

2. You need total cash (down payment +
   closing costs)   _____

3. You qualify for a gross income mortgage
   payment of: _____

   Or a net income mortgage payment of: _____

4. Your proposed mortgage payment would be: _____

If you don't qualify (line 4 exceeds either or both amounts on line 3) you need to do one of several things:

- Find a lower priced home.
- Increase your down payment.
- Try to arrange for better financing.
- Negotiate with the seller.

    NOTE: These formulas are for estimate purposes only, since different lenders use different formulas. Depending on the current supply of money, a lender may relax or increase its requirements. These changes can occur on a day-to-day basis.

    Important Point: Don't get over your head in mortgage payments because you fell in love with a home. There are more of them out there.

    Another Important Point: The CD-ROM gives you a quick, private estimate of how much house you can afford. Although it may be subject to revision by lenders' current methods of mortgage qualification, you will still have a good idea of what you can afford to buy.

GETTING PRE-QUALIFIED FOR A MORTGAGE

Before you start seriously looking for a home, professionals suggest that you meet with two or more lenders and get pre-qualified for a mortgage. Meeting with two or more lenders enables you to pick the best deal. Keep in mind that loans and loan qualification vary from lender to lender and on a day-to-day basis.

By being pre-qualified, you can confidently walk into any home and tell the owner that you are already pre-qualified by a lender. *This alone will give you a great deal of bargaining power with a seller* especially one who has had other offers fall apart because a buyer did not qualify for the loan.

When we talk about financing, we will cover mortgage qualification and working with lenders in more detail.

All right, you've done your homework. You have determined you can qualify for a $175,000 to $200,000 home. So . . . let's start looking, shall we?

HOW TO LOCATE YOUR HOME

Become familiar with the city. Get a feel for the neighborhoods you like. Are they in an appreciating area? Drive around and look at other homes on the street. Are they all in good repair and well maintained? You should also drive the adjoining areas. What surrounds the neighborhood you like? If it is bordered by a major highway, railroad, industrial park or other uses, you may want to think twice. You can hopefully find an area that is also surrounded by other residential neighborhoods.

Select the neighborhoods or subdivision that have homes in your price range. How do you know if the homes are in your price range? Call on a few signs in front of the homes that are of interest to you. If they are broker signs, you may have to do some talking in order to get a price out of the agent, but be persistent. Say that you don't want to waste anyone's time; you just happened to see the house and were curious about the price. It was mentioned in the seller section that a buyer who knows the location of the property and the price doesn't need the broker to decide if the home is worth considering. Fortunately for you, most brokers do not follow that basic rule. In an effort to please a caller, and hopefully get a live prospect, a broker will tell you anything you want to know. "For Sale By Owner" signs are usually easier. Unless the seller has read the same book you are reading now, you will readily find out everything you want to know about the house. If, after calling on three or four signs, you determine they are in your price range, start looking seriously.

Important Point: Do not eliminate any other areas for your consideration right now. If, for some reason, none of the homes in your original area are what you really want, you are going to be very unhappy. It's a good idea to have two or three neighborhoods on your list of possible locations. You may even determine that neighborhood number two or three will turn out to be a better choice than your first pick.

Practical Point: Every residential area is bordered by a "buffer." This buffer is generally zoned a "lower" use than the residential area. The most common buffer is apartment complexes. Then, between them and the major streets may be commercial properties such as office buildings and shopping centers. If you are looking at the last home before the primary buffer begins, you can expect to find apartments. If the land is zoned for industrial or something you consider to be undesirable, you need to move further into the subdivision or find a different area.

Make a note of For Sale By Owner (FSBO) signs on properties that look promising. Also include Realtor signs. You may need to work with one if all else fails. A Realtor will have access to most of the homes on the market through the MLS system. Homeowners often refuse to put out a sign in order to stop heavy broker traffic to their door.

Take pictures of those homes that are of interest. That way, once you get home and try to remember what a certain home looked like, you'll have photos of it. If you don't take pictures, by the time you get home after looking at a dozen or more homes, they all begin to look alike. If you have a digital camera and a computer, you can take digital images and download them directly into your computer for instant access. This will also let you preview what you have taken immediately, to be certain the picture clearly shows the home. No more waiting several days for the film to be developed and then discover that the house was sold in the interim.

Don't try to become a photo artist at this point. All you need is a photo to remind you of what the home looked like.

When you have covered the homes that are of interest, taken photos, and jotted down some notes about each, including the phone number on the sign, return home and review your list. You may try to put them in order of preference, but at this point, you don't know what they are like on the inside. That comes next.

Important Point: Make a list of questions you need immediate answers to before making any calls. Do not try to get all of your questions answered over the phone . . . just enough to know if the home is worth keeping on your list. These questions might include: How many bedrooms and baths? Has it been updated (on older homes)? The number of square feet (although most owners will not have the slightest idea of square footage)? Does it have a family or "great" room? In other words, ask any questions that would immediately eliminate the home from future consideration if that feature were not there.

MAKING APPOINTMENTS

You now have a list of several homes that are of interest. Start making phone calls to the homeowners. Make appointments to see several of your top choices. If the homes are close together, give yourself about twenty or thirty minutes between each appointment. Don't expect everyone to be home and ready to show the house. If a real estate agent has the home listed, you'll have to make an appointment through the realty office.

Begin, if you have a choice, by looking at non-real estate broker-listed homes. Your intention is to avoid paying a commission, so you don't want to get a broker involved at all. Even if you found the house on your own, an agent will expect to collect the entire commission on a broker-listed home, and will certainly not give you half because there was no other broker involved.

HOW TO FIND FSBOS

At this point you are no doubt thinking, "That's just great. I drove the entire neighborhood (s) for 'For Sale By Owner' signs and didn't find one. I do have a list of ten brokers though. What do I do now?"

Signs on properties are only one way to locate a FSBO. Many homeowners will not put a sign on a property because it invites all the neighbors and brokers in town to start bugging them. Instead, they will run ads in newspapers. If they are smart, they will have spelled out the subdivision or area of the city in which the home is located. If they are not so smart, they may even give the property address in the ad. That's all you need in order to drive by and take a look.

You can also check with the courthouse for foreclosures on properties. Lenders also have a list of properties they have foreclosed on. Quite often you can get a bargain property in a desirable area by following up on these contacts.

Using the Internet

The Internet is another great place to look for a home. There are literally thousands—even hundreds of thousands—of Web sites in which you can locate homes for sale. Concentrate on the many that offer FSBOs or homes for sale by owner. Many of the large sites allow you to pinpoint a specific city and location within that city. If you live in a large city, there will no doubt be many listed. You will find a list of Web sites on page 116, as well as on the CD-ROM that is included with this book. From the CD-ROM, you can access each site directly by clicking it on.

Important Point: The Internet listings of FSBOs give you two important features. First, you know the seller is serious about selling or would not have expended the time and money to list the home on the Internet. Second, most of these Internet listings will give you complete details on the property as well as the owner's name and address. (It's kind of like fishing out of a barrel.)

Other Ways to Find FSBOs

Don't overlook talking to people. Many times there are homeowners who want to sell but are not willing to commit to it with a sign or ad, knowing they will be besieged with calls if they do.

You can even run an ad stating that you are in the market for a three-bedroom home in a particular neighborhood and list any other feature you really need to have. Do not get too restrictive, however, or no one will call. One thing you need to do is mention in your ad that you are pre-qualified to buy a home in that area. Financing will be no problem. Secondly, do not reveal your price range. Remember, most sellers expect to negotiate on the price. If you say you want to buy a $150,000 home, a seller who knows the home is worth $200,000 won't call you. This may all end up with the acceptance of a $150,000 offer, especially from someone who the seller knows can afford to buy it. There is no way anyone will admit that until you begin negotiations.

WHAT TO LOOK FOR IN A HOME

You should prepare a profile of the kind of home you want, and what your home-buying objectives are. Use this to focus your search on homes that will be suitable for you. Consider the following:

__ Goals and Objectives: Why are you buying a home? What do you expect from it: A quiet place to live, room to "tinker," a yard for gardening, a pool, more room than you have now . . . less room than you have now, etc. Make a list of what you consider to be the minimum acceptable features.

__ Next, make a second list of "I'd like to have it if . . ." and include features that would be nice, if you can afford them and if they are available. Print out a copy of this checklist from the CD-ROM included with this book.

__ Location: Location is of primary importance when buying a home. What is the neighborhood like? Is it the kind of place you want to raise your children or retire, depending on your situation? Make certain the neighborhood is appreciating.

__ Physical Characteristics: The type of home that fits your needs and lifestyle: Split bedroom plan (where the master bedroom is on one side of the house and the other bedrooms are on the opposite side), large recreation or "great" room, number of bedrooms and baths. This is a "Must" list of things you really have to have.

__ Special Features: The special features that you want: Gourmet kitchen, ceiling fans, lots of large closets, pool, patio, hot tub, fireplace, laundry room, basement, attic for storage, garage (one- or two-car), etc.

__ Decorating: You'll never find the perfect home. You hope to find one that comes close to meeting your esthetic desires. How much redecorating will be required, or will you be able to live with it "as is" for a while? How about window treatments, carpet and tile? Are they acceptable as is? Many of these things can be changed a little at a time, if necessary. Will the home need repainting to make it livable?

__ The Exterior and Lot: Is the home on a reasonable size lot, or right next to the house next door? (Unless you are moving into a "zero lot line" community, it's nice to have some space between you and the neighbors.) Does it offer some privacy? What is the condition of the landscaping and lawn? How about the driveway, patio and other paved areas? Are they relatively free from cracks and potholes? How much exterior decorating will be required? Is the paint in good condition?

__ General Condition: You will have a formal inspection before closing to insure that appliances, water heater and heating/AC system are in working condition. You can, however, check for major structural cracks in outside walls and floors that are uneven. Visiting the home when it's raining is the best way to check for signs of roof leaks. If you find major problems, look for another home.

__ What About the Neighbors: Try to get an idea of what kind of neighbors you will have. If you can hear screaming fights going on next door, you may want to reconsider. One attorney advises to check a cross-reference phone book and get the names and addresses of the nearby neighbors. A quick check of the county records will tell you if any of them has a history of domestic violence, etc. (Use your judgment on this one.)

Use the Home Profile form on page 123 (and on the CD-ROM) to describe each home you see, and record your impressions and observations. You can also make up your own list of features you need to know about. It does not have to be fancy. Just hand write the information you need to know and make copies to use at each home you visit.

When touring the home, you want to take as many notes as you possibly can. (By the way, don't expect the sellers, who don't even know who you are, to allow you to take pictures inside their home.)

List what you like and do not like about the house. The more notes you take, the better the visual image will be of that house when you get home and start reviewing the several you toured. You may make comments like "huge gourmet kitchen with island" or "ugly purple draperies in living room." The fact that the house may have ugly purple draperies will not stop you from further consideration. It's just a way of remembering what you saw. You can always change the draperies.

Pay special attention to any defect you see. For example, normal exterior settling cracks in the foundation are normal. If, however, they are one-half inch wide, there may be a serious problem with the building. An even better example is uneven floors in a room. If the floor seems to slope downhill as you walk in, you'd better take a second look.

Check for signs of water leaks. Are there dark or wet spots in the ceiling or walls? One of the best times to look at a home is right after a heavy rainstorm, particularly an hour or so after it stops raining. If there are signs of roof leaks, they will be visible then. It will also give you a good indication of how well the drainage is off the property. If it is still under water an hour after the rain stops, there may be problems.

Important Point: Before you are firmly committed to buying a home, after you have an acceptable contract with the seller, you will want a full home inspection made. Many of these defects will be discovered at that time. The only purpose you have in making a list of defects on your initial visit is to eliminate any home that obviously will not pass the formal inspection. You want to be pretty certain the home you select and put under contract will pass an inspection with no major problems, because you are the one who pays for that inspection. You don't want to do that for three or four before you locate a home that has no major problems. This is the reason to discover them for yourself if you can.

Your checklist should also include any updating that has been done to the home. If it is twenty years old and still has the original kitchen equipment, heating/AC plant, water heater, etc., they are probably about ready to quit working. Do the kitchen or bathrooms need to be updated with new counters, fixtures, etc.? How about window treatments? It may not be exactly what you would have chosen, but is it acceptable for the time being? Although window treatments are a personal preference item, you need to consider anything you will want to change as a possible expense in the near future, and your initial offer to purchase should take this into consideration.

Important Point: Just because you do not like the color of the carpeting or the type of window treatments the present owner has, don't expect a big price cut because you want to replace it. When we discuss contract clauses, we'll also talk about inspections and the reasons for NOT using the word "satisfactory" when discussing the condition of appliances.

Another Important Point: Once you finally find the "perfect" home, DON'T LET THE SELLERS KNOW THIS! If you do, you have just lost all of your negotiating power. Wait until you are in your car and driving away before you let out that scream of joy. Why? If the seller thinks you really want the home, it will be much harder to negotiate a better price and other concessions.

Once you have found "the" home, sit down again and review all of the financing options you have and balance them against your budget. Also make a list of what you like and dislike about the home. Make certain the "likes" are not ruling your judgment. The "dislikes" should be minor things that are not critical and can be changed whenever you wish.

Before we cover preparing and negotiating a contract, we should look at other purchase options that may be open to you: Distressed Properties and Lease/Options. These two alternatives may be necessary if mortgage qualification is a problem.

SHOULD YOU CONSIDER BUYING A DISTRESSED PROPERTY?

Distressed properties are also known as "handyman specials." When you enter into a contract to buy this type of home, you should look for three things: good price, ability to upgrade, and good neighborhood.

Good Price: The home must be priced at below-market value for the area.

You will be required to spend money to put the home back in top condition. You'll want to make certain that, after spending money and time fixing it up, it will be worth the investment. For example, homes in the area are selling for $175,000. You can buy this one for $150,000 but will have to spend $30,000 to $40,000 to put it in the same condition as the comparable homes in the area. This does not make financial sense. If, however, you can buy it for $125,000 or less and put it in top condition for $30,000, you now have $155,000 invested in a home that has a fair market value of $175,000. Do your homework first. Why is the home in its present condition? Is there a problem with the home or the financial position of the owner?

Upgrading the Home: Can it be upgraded to bring it up to the value of other homes in the area? You need to be sure about this. We already discussed structural problems that cannot be cured or can only be cured at tremendous expense. You don't want to get into that situation.

Good Neighborhood: The home should be in a good neighborhood with quality homes. It is vitally important to insure that the other homes in the area are at least in the same or a higher price range as the one you are considering. If, for example, you end up with an upgraded home worth $175,000 and the highest price home in the neighborhood is only worth $125,000, you are overbuilt for the neighborhood.

Important Point: Never own the most expensive home on the street. The value of your expensive home will be downvalued to the level of the other homes.

Being successful at making money on "handyman specials" depends largely on your ability to know the market and understand what it will cost to fix up the home that is of interest.

One last point about "handyman specials." The best way to make money with a distressed home is if you do most of the repair work yourself. (That is commonly referred to as "sweat equity.") All the work you do yourself adds value to the home at no expense to you, except for supplies and the value of your time, and, if you have chosen the home wisely, you will be well paid for the updating.

Keep accurate records of everything you do to upgrade the home. Figure in not only the cost of materials but the value of your labor as well. What would it have cost you to hire a carpenter or plumber to do the work you did? This has several values to you.

- It may have a tax reduction value. Talk to your CPA about that.
- It is provable added value to the home.

- When you sell, you can show a potential buyer how much money you spent in upgrading the home after you bought it. An astute buyer may check the tax rolls to see how much you paid for the home. If the tax rolls show $125,000 and you are asking $175,000, a potential buyer will immediately think you are trying to make a killing. If, however, you can show paid bills (yes, including your charge for labor) and it can be seen that you spent $50,000 fixing it up, it will be assumed you are just trying to break even. Don't say that $40,000 of the $50,000 is your labor cost.

One more thing to do: Take pictures of the home, both inside and out, before you do any renovating. Pick the worst areas you can find for the photos. This will be especially important if you are trying to finance the home through a lender who is reluctant about letting you buy with a minimum down payment. Sit down with the lender and spread out the photos you have taken. Explain that it (the lender) currently owns a home in very distressed condition. The lender may not have actual title to the home, but it does have the majority of equity in it. If it does not let you buy it and fix it up, they may end up foreclosing on a home that is worth less than the mortgage. Believe me, any lender will listen to you. When we discuss financing, we will go into more detail on working with lenders.

If you are not a handyman or do not care to be one, you had better do your homework carefully. If you are paying to have everything done for you, your costs will probably at least triple. Make sure you do not end up overpaying for the home, after adding in the upgrade costs.

On the other hand, buying a distressed property and fixing it up yourself can result in a large profit. Once done, you can either sell it for a profit or have an upgraded home in which to live.

WHEN TO USE A LEASE/OPTION

What if you have decided that you want to buy a home but cannot qualify for a loan? You already know that you don't want to continue renting. What can you do? You can consider using a lease/option.

What is a lease/option and how does it work? Quite simply, the owner of the home rents the home to you and gives you an option to buy it at a later date. The reason? You cannot afford to buy the home now, but you will have the opportunity of accumulating equity in the home and buying it at a future date. That's the "Lease" part. What is the "Option" part? As you know, if you have an option to do something, that means you can do it or you don't have to do it. The same holds true here. Once you can afford to buy the home, you can decide if you want to do so.

Why would the seller go along with this? The owner could rent to you for two years or more and then end up getting the home back after you did who knows what to it. In order to purchase a home on a lease/option basis, you need to find a motivated seller. It has to be someone who needs to sell or who at least needs someone to make the mortgage payments. This is exactly what you will be doing: Your rent payments will cover the mortgage payments. Perhaps the owner has a second home and cannot afford two, or maybe is getting married and both partners own homes, but will only need one. This technique also works well when the market is slow and there are many homes on the market. The home you are considering has not sold and the seller is getting desperate. The home also may be distressed, which gives you a double opportunity to win at this game. You can build part of your equity with "sweat equity."

How It Works: You and the seller enter into a formal written agreement for a lease/option. You agree to pay so much a month in rental payments. The seller agrees to credit you with a portion of each rent payment toward a down payment on the home. If you agree to fix up the home, you will also be credited for the cost of the upgrading. You both agree that, when you have accumulated a certain amount of credits (equity), the owner will sign over the title of the home to you. You, in the initial agreement, also agreed to a selling price for the option to buy portion of the contract.

You will then have to qualify for the mortgage assumption, if there is one you can take over that is large enough to give the seller the agreed-upon price. If, for example, you agreed to pay $125,000 for the home and it has a $100,000 mortgage, you will need to accumulate $25,000 in equity through rent payment credits and repairs done to the home.

Another possibility is that the seller may be willing to carry a mortgage personally, once it is known that you are a reliable and conscientious homeowner. That gives you the best possible situation. Not only do you avoid mortgage qualifying with a lender, but you also save closing costs on the mortgage.

CAUTIONS AND SUGGESTIONS

Be certain to enter into a lease/option and not a lease/*purchase* agreement. A lease/purchase obligates you to buy the home at a later date, whether you want to or not, or lose any equity you build up during the past year or more of renting under the agreement. If you refuse to buy, or cannot afford to buy, you can be sued for "specific performance," if you happened to have a difficult seller.

Try to negotiate for the best possible price. Remember, the owner wants to get out from under the home for whatever the reason.

A lease/option has a big advantage in an appreciating market. You are entering into an agreement today for a possible closing of title a year or two or more down the road. In other words, you are able to tie up the property at today's prices for a closing in the future.

In the event you are unable or unwilling to close at the end of the option period, you can do one of two things. You can walk away from the property with no future obligation to do anything. Of course, you lose any money that was credited toward your down payment, but you would have been paying that in rent anyway. Second, you can try to obtain an extension on the option from the seller.

Important Point: You generally will not consider entering into a lease/option in the first place unless you have done your homework and know that this is the home you would like to buy, if you had the money to do so.

Don't expect to find many sellers willing to jump at the chance to sell to you on a lease/option basis. If homes are selling, there is little question that they would rather have an outright sale and not have to worry about a tenant. Here are the main reasons a lease/option will not work:

1. The seller needs the money out of this home to buy another.

2. There is no guarantee that you will pay rent each month, or do the repairs you promise; finally, you may not buy the home at all when

the option period expires. The seller is now back in the same position as a few years earlier, maybe worse.

3. The seller is not willing to sell you a home a year or two from now at today's prices.

4. There is always the hope that if the owner waits a little longer, a better offer will come in.

However, when you have little or no cash to put down, and you find a seller who will sell on a lease/option basis, it will give you a start toward home ownership. It may not be the home you want to end up with for ten years, but you at least have the chance to build equity.

FSBO WEB SITES

This is a brief list of For Sale By Owner Web sites. They are also on your CD-ROM. Insert the CD-ROM and you can click on them directly, once you are on line, to bring up each site. Some of the sites are large and allow you to select the city and state you want when you search.

www.fsbosites.com < http://www.fsbosites.com >
www.fsbonetwork.com < http://www.fsbonetwork.com >
www.fsbotips.com < http://www.fsbotips.com >
www.kcnet.com/ ~ phillips/fsbo/homefsbo.htm
    < http://www.kcnet.com/ ~ phillips/fsbo/homefsbo.htm >
www.hrfsbo.com/ < http://www.hrfsbo.com/ >
www.fsboworld.net < http://www.fsboworld.net >
www.homes.aolads.com < http://www.homes.aolads.com >
www.fsbocentral.com < http://www.fsbocentral.com >
www.mis-fsbo.com < http://www.mis-fsbo.com >
www.yourfsbo.com < http://www.yourfsbo.com >
www.visitourhome.com < http://www.visitourhome.com >
www.prescottvalley.net/advertising.html < http://www.prescottvalley.
    net/advertising.html >
www.geocities.com/TheTropics/Beach/9955/index.html
    < http://www.geocities.com/TheTropics/Beach/9955/index.html

www.fsbo.com < http://www.fsbo.com >
www.fsbo.net < http://www.fsbo.net >
www.braintaylor.com < http://www.braintaylor.com >
www.fisbos.com < http://www.fisbos.com >
www.4sale-byowners.com < http://www.4sale-byowners.com >
www.sanatoniofsbo.com < http://www.sanatoniofsbo.com >
www.tau.com < http://www.tau.com >
www.homes-of-florida.com < http://www.homes-of-florida.com >
www.chicagofsbo.net < http://www.chicagofsbo.net >
www.gulfcoastfotoads.com < http://www.gulfcoastfotoads.com >
www.idaho-fsbo.com < http://www.idaho-fsbo.com >
www.fsbofriend.com < http://www.fsbofriend.com >
www.realestatemd.com < http://www.realestatemd.com >
www.forsalebyowner.com < http://www.forsalebyowner.com >
www.realtytimes.com < http://www.realtytimes.com >
www.gwi.net < http://www.gwi.net >
www.webrealty.org.fsbo/fsbolisting.htm
    < http://www.webrealty.org.fsbo/fsbolisting.htm >
www.wegrew.com < http://www.wegrew.com >
www.onlineavenues.com < http://www.onlineavenues.com >
www.forsalebyownernetwork.com/contact.htm
    < http://www.forsalebyownernetwork.com/contact.htm >
www.3apes.com/business/classifieds < http://www.3apes.com/business/classifieds >
www.gmcmotorhome.com/fsbo/index.html
    < http://www.gmcmotorhome.com/fsbo/index.html >
www.monkeytool.com < http://www.monkeytool.com >
www.dir.infojump.com/dir/dmoz/business/classifieds
    < http://www.dir.infojump.com/dir/dmoz/business/classifieds >
www.buownersales.com < http://www.buownersales.com >
www.fsbo4bid.com/freebann.html < http://www.fsbo4bid.com/freebann.html >
www.pagedepot.com/business4u/salebusiness.html
    < http://www.pagedepot.com/business4u/salebusiness.html >

www.fsbohelp.com < http://www.fsbohelp.com >
www.housecenter.com/class/fsbo.htm
    < http://www.housecenter.com/class/fsbo.htm
www.fsbo-home.com < http://www.fsbo-home.com >
www.realestate4sale.com/infopages/advertise.asp
    < http://www.realestate4sale.com/infopages/advertise.asp >
www.fsbo-kiosk.com < http://www.fsbo-kiosk.com >
www.ushx.com < http://www.ushx.com >
www.owners.com < http://www.owners.com >
www.abilenefsbo.com < http://www.abilenefsbo.com >
www.fsbolistings.com < http://www.fsbolistings.com >
www.fsbohsr.com < http://www.fsbohsr.com >
www.sites.netscapt.net/jfhorse
    < http://www.sites.netscapt.net/jfhorse >
www.abetterfsbo.com < http://www.abetterfsbo.com >
www.usa4salebyowner.com < http://www.usa4salebyowner.com >
www.home-vue.com < http://www.home-vue.com >
www.old-houses.com < http://www.old-houses.com >
www.sell2all.com < http://www.sell2all.com >
www.wvare.net/more.html < http://www.wvare.net/more.html >
www.pennre.net < http://www.pennre.net >
www.arke.net < http://www.arke.net >
www.orere.net < http://www.orere.net >
www.rhodere.net < http://www.rhodere.net >
www.louisre.net < http://www.louisre.net >
www.oklare.net < http://www.oklare.net >
www.alaskare.net < http://www.alaskare.net >
www.ioware.net < http://www.ioware.net >
www.nordakre.net < http://www.nordakre.net >
www.wisre.net < http://www.wisre.net >
www.virgre.net < http://www.virgre.net >
www.ohiore.net < http://www.ohiore.net >

www.maryre.net < http://www.maryre.net >

www.privatelist.com/welcome.htm < http://www.privatelist.com/
welcome.htm >

www.members.home.net/vivwood/welcome.htm
< http://|www.members.home.net/vivwood/welcome.htm >

www.homeportfoliojunction.com < http://
www.homeportfoliojunction.com >

www.easyhomeseller.com/allabout.htm < http://www.easyhome-
seller.com/allabout.htm >

www.getfocused.com/promoter.htm < http://www.getfocused.com/
promoter.htm >

www.nfsboa.com < http://www.nfsboa.com >

www.fsbo.nebbadoon.com < http://www.fsbo.nebbadoon.com >

www.n-c-c.com/ < http://www.n-c-c.com/ >

www.jan.ucc.nau.edu < http://www.jan.ucc.nau.edu >

www.floidare.net < http://www.floidare.net >

www.kshin.com < http://www.kshin.com >

www.pin.ca/for_sale_by_owner/bc/default.htm
< http://www.pin.ca/for_sale_by_owner/bc/default.htm >

www.fsbonetwork.com < http://www.fsbonetwork.com >

www.io.com/house/depot.html
< http://www.io.com/house/depot.html >

www.insightful.net < http://www.insightful.net >

www.debtwoorkout.com/beta/rmli5.html < http://www.
debtwoorkout.com/beta/rmli5.html >

www.aktouch.com/fsbomac.htm < http://www.aktouch.com/
fsbomac.htm >

www.homesaledirect.com/help.cfm < http://www.homesaledirect.com/
help.cfm >

www.cswnet.com < http://www.cswnet.com >

www.fsbohunt.com < http://www.fsbohunt.com >

www.realweb.com < http://www.realweb.com >

www.houseexpress.com < http://www.houseexpress.com >

www.byowner.com < http://www.byowner.com >

www.homebytes.com < http://www.homebytes.com >

www.fsbolistingsusa.com < http://www.fsbolistingsusa.com >

www.rpmfind.net/ < http://www.rpmfind.net/ >

www.bargainhomes.com < http://www.bargainhomes.com >

www.fsbo-hsbay.com < http://www.fsbo-hsbay.com >

www.efsbo.com < http://www.efsbo.com >

www.gatewaytitle.com < http://www.gatewaytitle.com >

www.midland-homesbuyerowner.com < http://www.midland-homes-buyerowner.com

www.columpbiahomesforsale.com < http://www.columpbiahomesforsale.com >

www.uscounties.com/contact.html
   < http://www.uscounties.com/contact.html >

www.homead.com < http://www.homead.com

www.atlantafsbo.com/serv05.htm
   < http://www.atlantafsbo.com/serv05.htm >

www.webmasterinternational.com/4sale.htm
 < http://www.webmasterinternational.com/4sale.htm >

www.realestatenation.com/fsbo.htm
   < http://www.realestatenation.com/fsbo.htm >

www.list4free.com < http://www.list4free.com >

www.lifsbo.com < http://www.lifsbo.com >

www.webwombat.com < http://www.webwombat.com >

www.fsbokettlemoraine.com < http://www.fsbokettlemoraine.com >

www.houstonfsbo.com < http://www.houstonfsbo.com >

www.byowner.com < http://www.byowner.com >

www.losangelesfsbo.com < http://www.losangelesfsbo.com >

www.freeyellow.com < http://www.freeyellow.com >

www.dcfsbo.com < http://www.dcfsbo.com >

www.sandiegohomes4u.com < http://www.sandiegohomes4u.com >

www.dotcomusa.com < http://www.dotcomusa.com >

www.bigdfsbo.com < http://www.bigdfsbo.com >

www.mindspring.com/ ~jockamo3/index.html
    < http://www.mindspring.com/ ~jockamo3/index.html >

www.seattlefsbo.com < http://www.seattlefsbo.com

www.somd.com/classifieds/fsbo < http://www.somd.com/
    classifieds/fsbo >

www.carizona.com/fsbo/index.html < http://www.carizona.com/fsbo/
    index.html >

www.sandiegofsbo.com < http://www.sandiegofsbo.com >

www.comprealty.com < http://www.comprealty.com >

www.fsbo.prescottvalley.net < http://www.fsbo.prescottvalley.net >

www.kreick.com/fsboseattle.htm < http://www.kreick.com/
    fsboseattle.htm >

www.lifsbo.com < http://www.lifsbo.com >

www.encinohome4sale.com < http://www.encinohome4sale.com >

www.ucansellit.com < http://www.ucansellit.com >

www.fsboweb.com < http://www.fsboweb.com >

www.valuecom.com < http://www.valuecom.com >

www.david.hilton.net < http://www.david.hilton.net >

www.truckeetahoe.com < http://www.truckeetahoe.com >

www.newyorkfsbo.com < http://www.newyorkfsbo.com >

www.spriggsweb.com/fsbo_homes/fsbo_homes.html
    < http://www.spriggsweb.com/fsbo_homes/fsbo_homes.html >

www.motsbo.com < http://www.motsbo.com >

www.cloud9nc.com < http://www.cloud9nc.com >

www.fsboboston.com < http://www.fsboboston.com >

www.fastlane.net < http://www.fastlane.net >

www.gres.com < http://www.gres.com >

www.4cornersrealestate.com < http://www.4cornersrealestate.com >

www.showmeproperties.com/fsbo.htm < http://www.showmeproperties.
    com/fsbo.htm >

www.buyerbrokers.com < http://www.buyerbrokers.com >

www.all-connections.com/realestate/index.htm < http://www.all-connections.com/realestate/index.htm >

www.aaarealtyservices.com < http://www.aaarealtyservices.com >

www.njhomeguide.com < http://www.njhomeguide.com >

www.pathcom.com < http://www.pathcom.com >

www.philadelphiafsbo.com < http://www.philadelphiafsbo.com >

www.detroitfsbo.com < http://www.detroitfsbo.com >

www.tresinc.com < http://www.tresinc.com >

www.ownerlistings.com < http://www.ownerlistings.com >

www.brenda.be/ < http://www.brenda.be/ >

www.ired.com < http://www.ired.com >

www.fsboadvertisingservice.homepricecheck.com
    < http://www.fsboadvertisingservice.homepricecheck.com >

www.usellrealty.com < http://www.usellrealty.com >

NOTE: Checklist for Features I Would Like to Have If Affordable and Available to come.

Home Profile Form

Location of Home _____

Exterior Observations _____

_____

Contact Information _____

(The above three items can be filled in during your drive-by to select possibilities.)

Number of Bedrooms _____ Bathrooms _____

Family or Great Room _____ Formal Dining Room _____

Room Sizes: (If possible) BR1 _____ BR2 _____ BR3 _____

     Living Room _____ Family Room _____

     Kitchen _____

     Formal Dining Room _____ Other _____

Garage_____ Attic _____ Basement _____

Ceiling Fans _____ Appliances _____

Asking Price _____ Terms _____

Taxes _____ Are there any problems with the home?_____

_____

(Don't expect the seller to volunteer much here.)

Comments and Observations _____

_____

_____

_____

_____

CHAPTER 12

HOW TO PREPARE AND SUBMIT AN OFFER-TO-PURCHASE CONTRACT

You have found the home you want to buy. Now it's time to draw up an offer-to-purchase contract. If this is your first time buying a home, you may want some professional help or an attorney. Here is a set of rules to follow when preparing your offer.

RULE 1: Never make a verbal offer. The seller will not take you seriously and it will destroy your chances of making a written offer later. Suppose you want to buy a $175,000 home but are offering $150,000. If you just say you are willing to pay $150,000 for the home, the seller will probably tell you, "Put it in writing and I'll look at it."

RULE 2: Never offer full price unless the home is a real steal and will not last on the market. You need room to negotiate.

RULE 3: Make sure your contract gives you time to do what is necessary, like satisfying contingencies.

RULE 4: Be certain to include a clause allowing for home inspections—roof, termites, etc. Also be sure you have an "out" written into the contract if the inspection turns up major repair problems that cannot be resolved with the seller.

RULE 5: If applying for a new mortgage, be sure your contract includes a "cancellation without penalty" clause in the event you cannot secure one.

RULE 6: Although you want room to negotiate, don't make your offer so unrealistic that the seller will not take it seriously. You will lose any chance of entering into negotiations.

MAKING A DEPOSIT WITH AN OFFER

Ideally you will be asked to put down a ten percent deposit. On a $150,000 home, that would be $15,000. Some buyers do not understand the reason for a large deposit. If you put up only $500 with your contract, the seller will feel insecure about your offer. Should you decide not to buy the home, the seller will keep your deposit (with some exceptions). You probably would not mind losing $500, if you had a good reason not to close on the purchase of the home. Perhaps you found another one you like better. The seller, however, only has $500 to show for the time the property was taken off the market. In the meantime, word will have spread that the home is under contract and would-be buyers will disregard it. The seller will have lost at least a month of selling time. Even worse, the home has been officially "off the market" and marketing efforts must begin again. Some buyers who knew the home was under contract will shy away from it now because they feel there was a reason the previous buyer decided not to buy. There must be something wrong with it.

A buyer who has $15,000 at stake is not likely to walk away from the purchase because the entire $15,000 could be lost. But you don't have to put down the entire $15,000 with the original offer. In fact, a buyer usually puts up a small deposit with a contract to purchase and specifies that an additional deposit will be added within a certain number of business days, after the contract has been agreed to and executed by all parties. This helps a buyer who does not want to tie up that large sum of money until the contract is acceptable to the seller. However, there are some exceptions to this.

Most contracts include certain clauses that offer "outs" in case the buyer is *unable* to close. Notice I said, "unable." Perhaps the buyer did not qualify for a mortgage. The contract clause spelling out the mortgage contingency must make it clear that "If the buyer, after diligent efforts, cannot qualify for a mortgage, the deposit shall be refunded to the buyer and liability on all parties shall cease." Again, the wording of that clause specifies that there must be a "diligent" effort to secure a mortgage. A buyer who decides not to buy the home cannot just refuse to apply for a mortgage and use that clause as an "out."

EXCEPTIONS TO THE TEN-PERCENT-DOWN RULE

A contract can be written any way a buyer and seller agree upon. If the seller is satisfied with a small deposit, there is nothing wrong with it. In some states, there must be some type of "consideration" included with a contract or it is not a valid offer to purchase. Here's another interesting twist. Suppose you do not have ready cash for a $15,000 deposit. You do, however, have something else of value—a car, stock, CDs. There are no rules stating you cannot use something other than cash as collateral. You may even give the seller a second mortgage on another property you own. If, of course, you put up the cash, the other collateral will be returned to you.

WHAT HAPPENS TO YOUR DEPOSIT?

Any money you deposit with a contract is held in an "escrow" or a "trust" account by the party you have handling the closing. It may be an attorney or a title company. That money cannot be touched until a closing takes place or the contract is cancelled. If the contract is cancelled, all parties must agree to and execute a release of deposit document showing who gets what portion of the money. This is where both buyer and seller must agree that the contract was cancelled due to no fault of the buyer—such as the buyer could not qualify for a mortgage. If, however, the buyer wants to cancel the contract because another house is preferred, the problem becomes a matter of arbitration between the parties to settle what happens to that deposit. You must realize that you could lose all or part of that deposit or be sued for specific performance (taken to court and required to close on the purchase). On the other hand, the seller must decide if it is worth the time and expense to force the sale.

The important point is that the deposit cannot be released from escrow until both parties agree in writing as to how that money will be released.

The escrow agent will collect a fee for handling the closing plus any other closing costs that must be paid, such as recording of the deed, etc.

INTEREST-BEARING ESCROW ACCOUNTS

You will be tying up a sizable amount of money for a few months, waiting until the closing on the property. Since you will no doubt be losing interest on those funds, you can generally request their deposit in an interest-bearing escrow account. Since people rarely make this request, the escrow agent may not have such an account already setup and may not be too willing to establish one just for you, but you have every right to request it. The exception would be if you stand to lose only a few dollars while that money is being held. It will probably cost the escrow agent more to set up the account than what you will collect in interest for that month or two.

Important Point: Do not write a contract too specific so that almost any variance from what is written can be used as an "out." Sellers, if they know anything at all, will quickly reject any such offers. Conversely, nothing is written in stone. There is no reason why you and the seller cannot get together and work out problems that may come up that will stop you from closing on the purchase. It may even be a reduction in price to compensate for a major problem the home inspector discovered. The seller, if this type of situation arises, must consider the consequences if you cannot be satisfied. The home is back on the market and a month or more of marketing time has been lost. Probably one or more potential buyers has also been lost during that time. The seller who is waiting to close on this home in order to buy another one that is under contract could have real problems. So for the benefit of both the buyer and the seller—be willing to work out any difficulties that come up between the contract stage and the actual closing.

See the Real Estate Sale and Purchase Contract on pages 137–144. It is a general form that can probably be used in most states, but you should consult with an attorney to be sure it's acceptable and valid in your area. Take the time to read the entire contract and become familiar with what is contained in it. Most of the items are self-explanatory.

CONTRACT BASICS

A contract may seem a somewhat formidable document, but it really only consists of a few main parts:

1. The first few lines identify the buyer, seller, and the property. The property is identified, not only by the address but by two additional methods. The first is the "legal description." That is the identification used to distinguish that particular piece of property from every other one in the entire country. No two legal descriptions are alike. It usually looks something like: Lot 23, Block 12 of Fair Acres section 3 as recorded in plat book 45 on page 80 of Our county. The plat book is the recorded "map" of every parcel of land in the county. The second identification number is the one used by the county tax assessor's office which looks something like this: 23-12-34-41-84-003. We won't go into what each group of numbers represents but if you look at your tax bill you will see similar numbers for your property ID.

   This section also contains a list of personal property or "not attached" items that will be included in the purchase. If the inventory list is too long to fit in the box, the normal procedure is to attach, as an addendum, a personal property list. The wording in that box will then be something like this: "An addendum of personal property is attached to and a part of this contract. See Addendum I." (Again, check to verify the acceptable wording for your area.) Both the contract and the addendum need to be dated and signed by both buyer(s) and seller(s).

2. The next section of the contract spells out the price and terms of the offer to purchase, including any mortgages that will be involved. It also outlines how the deposit will be paid and who will hold it.

Important Point: This is where complete detail on the mortgage to be assumed or to be applied for must be spelled out. (See the section on Mortgages for information on how to word the mortgage contingency in your contract.) You want to protect yourself, but at the same time do not make the criteria for obtaining a new mortgage so restrictive that it is really nothing more than an escape clause if you want "out" of the contract. Most sellers will recognize this and automatically reject your offer.

3. The next section is the most comprehensive. It spells out everything that needs to be said or done concerning the purchase and sale of the property. Included are inspections, title and deed information, remedies for default, liens, who pays for what, prorations, etc. The list is lengthy. Again, it is a good idea to at least familiarize yourself with the information outlined in the contract.

    Important Point: Once this document is executed by all parties, it becomes legal and binding. If you have any uncertainties about what you are filling in and signing, you need to seek legal counsel. Unfortunately, you will no doubt be charged to prepare a whole new contract, which will be almost like the one you already have, but knowing you have legal advice will remove some of the fear of doing it on your own.

4. The next section allows room for special clauses that are not pre-printed in the form contract. NOTE: Any clause that is written into a contract supersedes the pre-printed portion that it clarifies or changes. If you have too many special clauses to fit in the box provided, you can attach a separate "Addendum" form to the main contract. Make sure it is dated and refers to the original contract, identifying the parties to the transaction and the property address and legal description.

5. The final section of the contract spells out a time for its acceptance by the seller. You want to keep this as short as possible. Sometimes this can happen right after you make the offer; quite often, it will not happen that soon. The seller may want some time to think about

it or to discuss it with an attorney. But you want a time limit for acceptance. Try to get a decision from the seller within twenty-four hours or less. If you leave the time framework too long, the seller will have the opportunity to "shop" your contract, which means using your contract to get a better offer from someone else who might be waiting in the wings.

Next, if a broker was involved, the real estate commission is spelled out here and the broker's company name identified.

Finally, the signature lines for both buyer and seller, with the date each signed. It also includes lines for the buyer's and seller's Tax ID or social security numbers. (Yes, IRS will be informed of the transaction.)

CONTRACT CLAUSES YOU NEED TO KNOW ABOUT

Here are several contract clauses that you need to become familiar with and use when appropriate. Some of them are already written into the sample contract and others are often overlooked, but vitally important to you.

Inspection Clauses

Your contract will include inspection clauses that allow you, at your expense, to have the home inspected for anything that needs to be repaired or replaced. Your contract spells out how much of this work is the seller's responsibility. If the home is in drastic need of repairs, you can expect the seller to allow only a certain percentage of the purchase price for repairs or let it be understood that "the house is being sold in an 'as is' condition." It will then be up to you to decide if repairs will add too much to the cost of the house to make it a wise investment.

Mortgage Verification

Quite often, the information quoted by a seller regarding the current mortgage balance, terms and conditions varies greatly from what the actual numbers will be when the title is transferred. You need to know, well before the closing, if there are problems in accepting the actual mortgage terms and conditions. You may discover that the mortgage balance is $8,243 less than you were told it would be. This means you will need an additional $8,243 to close on the property. If you don't have it to pay, some other arrangement will have to be made. Get the seller to carry a short-term second mortgage for the difference. Better yet, get the price lowered accordingly.

Writing a Mortgage Clause

This is subject to your legal counsel's advice. The common method is to state that the buyer has fifteen working days, from the executing of this contract, in which to obtain a mortgage commitment in the amount of $100,000, or any other amount agreed to, at current rate and terms. The buyer further agrees to apply for a mortgage in a timely and diligent manner.

Let's dissect that statement. A time limit has been established for obtaining a mortgage (15 working days). The amount has been specified at $100,000 but leaves the door open to "any other amount agreed to." The buyer may be willing to accept $95,000 if that is all the lender will give. In any event, the contract does not automatically die if the purchaser can only obtain a $95,000 mortgage. When we discuss financing, you will learn how a seller can enter into the picture in this situation and help save the transaction. Next, instead of spelling out a certain interest rate and term, the contract specifies current rate and terms. Interest rates and terms vary from lender to lender and day to day. You don't want a contract to fall apart because the lender wants an extra quarter of a percent interest rate.

The "Sale-of-Your-Home" Contingency

Perhaps you have found the ideal home and make an offer to purchase on it. There is one problem, however: You need the money from the sale of your home and you haven't closed yet. You can make an offer to purchase, subject to the sale and closing on your home. If your home does not sell within a specified time, you can cancel the contract on the home you want to buy. What you need to understand is that the seller of the home you want probably will not like that contingency. After all, the seller will not know if the home is really sold until you state in writing that you have closed on your home and have removed that contingency on the contract. A seller who is really desperate to sell may consider accepting a "sale of your home first" contingency, but most will not.

There are two different variables here. If you already have a firm contract on your present home and all contingencies on your contract have been satisfied (your buyer is just waiting to close and all inspections, mortgage contingency, etc., have been satisfied), you will be in a much stronger position. If, however, you do not have a buyer on a contract or you have a contract loaded with contingencies, don't expect the seller to welcome your offer.

PRESENTING YOUR OFFER

You worked very hard to do your research for a home, select the right home, gather all of the information and prepare a formal offer to purchase. You are now sitting with the seller(s) prepared to make your offer. In the back of your mind, you already know what the objections will be and also the agreement points. We'll assume you are offering $150,000 for the home that is being offered at $185,000. From your research, you know the home is really only worth $175,000.

Begin your presentation by getting the seller to nod "'yes." "I'd like to have a home inspection done on your home." "Yes, that's fine." "I need to apply for a mortgage, but I'm already pre-qualified for it." "Yes, that's good." "I have a deposit check here for $1,000 and will increase it to ten percent of the price as soon as we have a signed contract." Go through anything you added to the contract that you feel certain will get a nod "Yes." Then calmly mention that you are offering $150,000 for the home. The head(s) may stop nodding "yes" but that thought is still there. "This buyer is already qualified for the mortgage; it is the only offer we've had."

Hand over a copy of the contract once you have made your entire presentation and then do the hardest part of the negotiation process . . . shut up and wait. Do not say another word. There is an old saying that the first person who talks, loses!

I've seen some buyers, and brokers, who never quit talking. The sellers never have a chance to think about the offer and make a decision.

Don't fall into that trap. You may not win them all, but you are sure to lose if you can't quit talking after making your presentation. The sellers need time to think about it.

So you sit there and sit there, if you are lucky. The other alternative is to have the seller hand back the contract immediately and tell you to "get realistic." The longer the owner sits, the more chance you have of winning . . . and that's what it's all about. You are sure you are sitting there for ten minutes and no one has spoken and you know that the first one who talks loses. While making a presentation one day, I decided to time that unbelievably long silence. After what seemed like an eternity, the seller finally spoke. I glanced at my watch and we had only been in silence for one and one-half minutes—ninety seconds.

The seller finally says, "This price is not acceptable." . . . Surprise, we already knew that. We also knew (and so did the seller) that we expected to have to increase our offering price. The seller finally says, "I'll take $170,000 for my home and not a penny less." Now it's your turn to let the seller stew while you decide what you want to do. You have an advantage over the seller, however, because you were prepared for this. After a few minutes, you say, "I'll increase my offer to $167,000." Now you are only $3,000 apart. Unless the seller has a better offer somewhere, you have a deal. And you are getting the home for about $8,000 less than market value.

SIGNING ON THE DOTTED LINE

Once you have both agreed, cross out any items that need changing and both you and the seller(s) must initial every change that was made.

Once everything is signed, leave a copy of the contract with the seller, ask any questions you may have and, finally, thank the seller for cooperating. Explain that you will communicate regularly about inspections, financing, added deposit being made, etc. Leave telephone numbers where you can be reached. It's time to leave. This is not the time or place to have a social hour. It will be difficult to keep that broad grin from your face as you back out of the driveway and know that you have just successfully found, negotiated a purchase for, and bought a home . . . without any help from a broker.

COUNTER OFFERS AND COUNTER-COUNTER OFFERS

I know, you're confused. Let's explain what is going on here. You submit an offer-to-purchase to the seller. The seller finds the price, terms, and/or some other items unacceptable as is. So the seller counter offers. This is done by crossing out the item(s) to be changed, making the changes on the contract, and *initialing each change.* You also need to make certain that the contract is executed by all parties complete with social security number and date it is executed. The signature lines are usually at the bottom of the last page.

Important Point: It is vitally important that each change in the contract be initialed by each party to the transaction.

Another Important Point: It is also a good idea to have all parties initial each page to show that they have read and understood it. This includes any "addendum" pages, such as a personal property inventory page, that may have been added to the basic contract. This insures that all parties to the contract are aware of and agree to each page of the completed contract.

Once all parties have done all of the initialing and signing, it makes additional negotiation much less painful. All the contract needs for any added changes is the initials of all parties next to the change.

Now you get the revised contract for review. You do not like some of the changes. Why? Because they are not the ideal price or terms you had originally hoped to obtain. Now you want to make some changes, usually trying to reach some type of an agreement between what you want and what the seller wants. You now make a counter-counter offer by crossing out the changes made by the seller and writing in the revised ones. Again, each change must be initialed.

The seller may agree to the counter-counter offer or make yet some more changes. Again the same process takes place. As you can see, there can be many changes made on a contract and you begin to have trouble figuring out what is what. Which ones are the most recent changes?

One way to keep them straight is to use a different colored pen for each set of changes. The first may be in black ink (the main contract is typewritten). It is also initialed with a black pen. The counter-counter offer changes may be made and initialed in blue ink, the next set in red, etc. You now have an easy way to identify which changes are the most recent and, more important, that all parties to the contract have initialed the most recent changes.

WHY NOT PREPARE A NEW CONTRACT?

By the time you reach agreement with the seller, there could be quite a few changes made to the contract. Items have been crossed out, changed, and initialed. There is no question that it can become confusing, which is a reason we suggested using a different colored pen for each change. Wouldn't it be easier to start with a fresh contract?

The name of the game is to get both parties to agree to a compromise as quickly and painlessly as possible. In other words, "Let's not start this whole process all over again!" Suppose you reach the point where the original selling price of $150,000 has been reduced by the original offer to $135,000. The seller counter offered at $145,000. At this point, neither party has what was originally wanted. With every change after that, both parties are giving up something. If you prepare a new contract with each change, both parties must execute the bottom of the contract and initial each page. They are now starting from the beginning with a contract price and terms that are less than either of them wanted.

It is much easier to get initials on changes than to get a whole new contract signed, once changes have been made. Once both parties have agreed to all the terms and conditions, changes made on the contract and initialed by all parties, you have a binding contract. Now may be the time to prepare a fresh contract so the closing agent can read what the parties have negotiated.

It is easier to get that fresh contract completed now because there is an underlying one that has been executed and agreed to. The name of the game is to get a written agreement between the buyer and seller. The fewer obstacles you face, the easier it will be.

THE WALKTHROUGH INSPECTION

You will usually have two inspections of the home jointly with the seller.

The first inspection takes place at the time a contract is executed. Both you and the seller have agreed not only on price and terms, but you have satisfied yourself that the home is what you want. This also includes the décor that stays with the home—draperies, ceiling fans, washer and dryer, etc. The subject of having an inventory of personal property was covered in Chapter 5. That inventory will include more than personal property, which consists of personal items that are not attached to the building or walls. It may also cover items that are attached that would not normally be considered "personal property" but the seller wants to keep them. When making your inspection of the property, prior to writing up a contract, make a list of items you find are not right, such as visible leaks, dripping water faucets, etc. A checklist is included on page 147 to remind you of what to look for.

So you now have a firm contract that spells out all the terms and conditions of the purchase of the property. Attached to and a part of that contract is the inventory of personal property that both you and seller have agreed to. You have toured the home and are satisfied with what you have seen. The only exceptions may be necessary repairs that the seller has agreed to resolve. It may also include any repairs needed as a result of the roof, termite, appliance and general inspection that was or will be completed.

Let's assume everything has gone the way it should and it is now the day of closing, a month later. Now it is time for the second walkthrough inspection of the home. You and the seller, prior to attending the closing of title, make another joint inspection. The purpose is to make certain the home is in the same or better condition as it was on the day the contract was signed. The floors have been "broom cleaned," everything that is to be moved has been removed from the premises, and all the personal property that was supposed to remain is there. Once everyone is satisfied with the walkthrough, the closing can take place.

If both parties have lived up to their part of the agreement, the walkthrough should be no more than a formality.

Sample Real Estate Sale and Purchase Contract

_____, of _____ as Seller, and

_____, of _____ as Buyer,

hereby agree that the Seller shall sell and the Buyer shall buy the following described property UPON THE TERMS AND CONDITIONS HEREINAFTER SET FORTH, which shall include the STANDARDS FOR REAL ESTATE TRANSACTIONS set forth within this contract.

1. **LEGAL DESCRIPTION** of real estate located in _____ County, State of _____ together with all improvements and attached items, including fixtures, built-in appliances, attached wall-to-wall carpeting, draperies, rods and window coverings. The other items included in the purchase price are:

_____

The following items are excluded from the purchase:

_____

2. **PURCHASE PRICE** $ _____

Dollars.

Method of Payment:

(a) Deposit to be held in trust by: $

_____   _____

(b) Additional Deposit due within _____ days $ _____

(c) Approximate principal balance of first
    mortgage to which conveyance shall be
    subject, if any, to Mortgage Lender: $

Interest _____ % per annum:

    Method of payment: _____

(d) Other_____ $ _____

(e) Balance to close with cashier's check. $ _____

continued . . .

3. **FINANCING:** If the purchase price or any part of it is to be financed by a third-party loan, this Contract is conditioned on Buyer obtaining a written commitment within ___ days after Effective Date for (CHECK ONLY ONE): ___a fixed; ___an adjustable; or ___ a fixed or adjustable rate loan for the principal amount of $_____, at an initial interest rate not to exceed _____%, and a term of _____ years. Buyer will make application within _____ days after Effective Date and use reasonable diligence to obtain the loan commitment and, thereafter, to satisfy the terms and conditions of the commitment and close the loan. Buyer shall pay all loan expenses. If Buyer fails to obtain the commitment under this subparagraph within the time for the commitment of the terms and conditions of the commitment, then either party, by written notice to the other, may cancel this Contract and Buyer shall be refunded the deposit(s).

4. **CLOSING DATE:** This contract shall be closed and the deed and possession shall be delivered on or before the _____ ___A.M. ___P.M., on the _____ day of _____, _____, unless extended by other provisions of this contract.

5. **PRORATIONS:** Taxes, insurance, interest, rents and other expenses and revenue of said property shall be prorated as of the date of closing.

6. **PLACE OF CLOSING:** Closing shall be held at the office of the Seller's attorney or as otherwise agreed upon.

7. **TIME IS OF THE ESSENCE:** Time is of the essence for this Sale and Purchase Agreement.

Buyer (___) (___) and Seller (___) (___) acknowledge receipt of a copy of this page, which is page 1 of 4 pages.

continued . . .

8. RESTRICTIONS, EASEMENTS, LIMITATIONS: Buyer shall take title subject to: (a) Zoning, restrictions, prohibitions and requirements imposed by governmental authority, (b) Restrictions and matters appearing on the plat or common to the subdivision, (c) Public utility easements of record, provided said easements are located on the side or rear lines of the property, (d) Taxes for year of closing, assumed mortgages, and purchase money mortgages, if any, (e) Other: _____. Seller warrants that there shall be no violations of building or zoning codes at the time of closing.

9. DEFAULT BY BUYER: If Buyer fails to perform any of the covenants of this contract, all money paid pursuant to this contract by Buyer as aforesaid shall be retained by or for the account of the Seller as consideration for the execution of this contract and, as agreed, liquidated damages and in full settlement of any claims for damages.

10. DEFAULT BY SELLER: If the Seller fails to perform any of the covenants of this contract, the aforesaid money paid by the Buyer, at the option of the Buyer, shall be returned to the Buyer on demand; or the Buyer shall have only the right of specific performance.

11. TERMITE INSPECTION: At least 15 days before closing, Buyer, at Buyer's expense, shall have the right to obtain a written report from a licensed exterminator stating that there is no evidence of live termite or other wood-boring insect infestation on said property nor substantial damage from prior infestation on said property. If there is such evidence, Seller shall pay up to three (3%) percent of the purchase price for the treatment required to remedy such infestation, including repairing and replacing portions of said improvements which have been damaged; but if the costs for such treatment or repairs exceed three (3%) percent of the purchase price, Buyer may elect to pay such excess. If Buyer elects not to pay, Seller may pay the excess or cancel the contract.

12. ROOF INSPECTION: At least 15 days before closing, Buyer, at Buyer's expense, shall have the right to obtain a written report from a licensed roofer stating that the roof is in a watertight condition. In the event repairs are required either to correct leaks or to replace damage to fascia or soffit, Seller shall pay up to three (3%) percent of the purchase price for said repairs which shall be performed by a licensed roofing contractor; but if the costs for such repairs exceed three (3%) percent of the purchase price, Buyer may elect to pay such excess. If Buyer elects not to pay, Seller may pay the excess or cancel the contract.

continued . . .

13. OTHER INSPECTIONS: At least 15 days before closing, Buyer or his agent may inspect all appliances, air conditioning and heating systems, electrical systems, plumbing, machinery, sprinklers and pool system included in the sale. Seller shall pay for repairs necessary to place such items in working order at the time of closing. Within 48 hours before closing, Buyer shall be entitled, upon reasonable notice to Seller, to inspect the premises to determine that said items are in working order. All items of personal property included in the sale shall be transferred by Bill of Sale with warranty of title.

14. MECHANICS' LIENS: Seller shall furnish to Buyer an affidavit that there have been no improvements to the subject property for 90 days immediately preceding the date of closing, and no financing statements, claims of lien or potential liens known to Seller. If the property has been improved within that time, Seller shall deliver releases or waivers of all mechanics' liens as executed by general contractors, subcontractors, suppliers and material men, in addition to the Seller's lien affidavit, setting forth the names of all general contractors, subcontractors, suppliers and material men and reciting that all bills for work to the subject property which could serve as basis for mechanics' liens have been paid or will be paid at closing time.

15. DOCUMENTS FOR CLOSING: Seller's attorney shall prepare deed, note, mortgage, Seller's affidavit, any corrective instruments required for perfecting the title, and closing statement and submit copies of same to Buyer's attorney, and copy of closing statement to the broker, at least two days prior to scheduled closing date.

16. EXPENSES: State documentary stamps required on the instrument of conveyance and the cost of recording any corrective instruments shall be paid by the Seller. Documentary stamps to be affixed to the note secured by the purchase money mortgage, intangible tax on the mortgage, and the cost of recording the deed and purchasing money mortgage shall be paid by the Buyer.

Buyer (___) (___) and Seller (___) (___) acknowledge receipt of a copy of this page, which is page 2 of 4 pages

continued . . .

17. INSURANCE: If insurance is to be prorated, the Seller shall, on or before the closing date, furnish to Buyer all insurance policies or copies thereof.

18. RISK OF LOSS: If the improvements are damaged by fire or casualty before delivery of the deed and can be restored to substantially the same condition as now within a period of 60 days thereafter, Seller shall so restore the improvements and the closing date and date of delivery of possession hereinbefore provided shall be extended accordingly. If Seller fails to do so, the Buyer shall have the option of (1) taking the property as is, together with insurance proceeds, if any, or (2) canceling the contract, and all deposits shall be forthwith returned to the Buyer and all parties shall be released of any and all obligations and liability.

19. MAINTENANCE: Between the date of the contract and the date of closing, the property, including lawn, shrubbery and pool, if any, shall be maintained by the Seller in the condition as it existed as of the date of the contract, ordinary wear and tear excepted.

20. LEASES: Seller, not less than 15 days before closing, shall furnish to Buyer copies of all written leases and estoppel letters from each tenant specifying the nature and duration of the tenant's occupancy, rental rates and advanced rent and security deposits paid by tenant. If Seller is unable to obtain such letters from tenants, Seller shall furnish the same information to Buyer within said time period in the form of a Seller's affidavit, and Buyer may contact tenants thereafter to confirm such information. At closing, Seller shall deliver and assign all original leases to Buyer.

21. OTHER AGREEMENTS: No agreements or representations, unless incorporated in this contract, shall be binding upon any of the parties.

22. RADON GAS DISCLOSURE: Radon is a naturally occurring radioactive gas that, when it has accumulated in a building in sufficient quantities, may present health risks to persons who are exposed to it over time. Levels of radon that exceed Federal and State guidelines have been found in Florida buildings. Additional information regarding radon and radon testing may be obtained from your county public health unit. Buyer may, within the inspection period, have a licensed person test the property for radon. If radon exceeds the accepted level, seller may choose to reduce the level to an acceptable EPA level or either party may cancel the contract if the Seller fails to comply.

continued . . .

23. LEAD PAINT HAZARD: Every purchaser of any interest in residential real property on which a residential dwelling was built prior to 1978 is notified that such property may present exposure to lead from lead-based paint that may place young children at risk of developing lead poisoning. Lead poisoning in young children may produce permanent neurological damage, including learning disabilities, reduced intelligence quotient, behavioral problems and impaired memory. Lead poisoning also poses a particular risk to pregnant women. The Seller of any interest in residential real estate is required to provide the Buyer with any information on lead-based paint hazards from risk assessments or inspection in the Seller's possession and notify the Buyer of any known lead-based paint hazards. A risk assessment or inspection for possible lead-based paint hazards is recommended prior to purchase.

24. TYPEWRITTEN OR HANDWRITTEN PROVISIONS: Typewritten or handwritten provisions inserted in this form shall control all printed provisions in conflict therewith.

25. SPECIAL CLAUSES: _____

_____

26. The Following Addenda shall be attached to and become part of this contract:

_____

RIDERS: Check those that apply and are attached to this contract:

____Condominium Rider; ____Lead Paint Disclosure; ____Agency Disclosure (brokers);

____"As Is" Rider; ____Other _____

DISCLOSURES: Buyer ____acknowledges *or* ____ does not acknowledge receipt of above Riders.

Buyer (___) (___) and Seller (___) (___) acknowledge receipt of a copy of this page, which is page 3 of 4 pages

continued . . .

COMMISSION TO BROKER: The Seller hereby recognizes _____ as the Broker in this transaction, and agrees to pay as commission _____% of the gross sales price, or the sum of _____ Dollars ($_____) or one-half of the deposit in case same is forfeited by the Buyer through failure to perform, as compensation for services rendered, provided same does not exceed the full amount of the commission.

DEPOSIT RECEIPT

Deposit received by: (Print) _____ (Signature) _____

The above individual received the amount specified in Paragraph 2(a) on _____, _____.

TIME FOR ACCEPTANCE OF OFFER

Buyer offers to purchase the Property on the above terms and conditions. Unless this contract is accepted by the Seller and a copy delivered to the Buyer no later than _____ ___A.M. ___P.M. on _____, ____, this contract may be revoked at Buyer's option, and Buyer's deposit refunded subject to clearance of funds.

BUYER

Date: _____ Buyer: _____ Tax ID No. _____

Date: _____ Buyer: _____ Tax ID No. _____

Phone: _____ Address: _____

Fax: _____

continued . . .

SELLER

Date: _____ Seller: _____ Tax ID No. _____

Date: _____ Seller: _____ Tax ID No. _____

Phone: _____ Address: _____

Fax: _____

**Company Name and address
(If applicable)**

No representation as to the legal validity or adequacy of any provision of this form is made. If you have questions, seek legal counsel prior to executing any contract.

Buyer (___) (___) and Seller (___) (___) acknowledge receipt of a copy of this page, which is page 4 of 4 pages.

BUYER CONTRACT CLAUSES

NOTE: These contract clauses are not intended to be used without review by legal counsel. They are here to remind you of what needs to be included in a contract that many pre-printed contracts omit.

__ *Terms:* Terms of any mortgage must be spelled out entirely. These include: Mortgage Balance, Remaining Term, Interest Rate, Balloon Amount and Due Date if any, monthly P & I Payments, Terms of Assumption, etc.

__ *Title:* The seller must furnish a "marketable title," free and clear of any debt, except as noted and agreed to.

__ *Assumed Mortgage:* Spell out the complete terms and condition of any mortgage you are assuming and remedies if there are problems with it. Spell out the balance to be assumed. *Include a clause that will require the seller to carry any deficiency in the form of a second mortgage.* (Example: You intend to assume an existing $100,000 mortgage and find out at closing that the remaining balance is only $95,000. You must come up with additional $5,000 cash at closing. Have your contract written that the seller will carry this amount in the form of a second mortgage.)

__ *Inspections:* A time limit for any inspections must be in writing. Spell out what inspections are needed: Roof, Termite, Appliances, etc. You may want to employ an inspection company to do a complete inspection.

__ *Repairs:* The contract should specify how repairs are to be handled. Most contracts allow for a percentage of the purchase price to cover repairs that are the seller's responsibility.

__ *Leases:* If the property is leased, the seller will sign over any leases to you at closing. If you are leasing the property, you should verify the amount and terms of the lease with the tenant.

__ *Mechanics Liens:* A clause protecting the buyer from any liens that may surface should be included in the contract. The seller will furnish you with a "no-lien" affidavit.

__ *Closing Costs:* A clause spells out which closing costs are the buyer's responsibility. You should expect a copy of the closing statement well prior to closing in order to review your costs and be prepared to pay them.

__ *Taxes, Insurance and Escrow Account Balances:* If you are assuming a mortgage, there will no doubt be an escrow account to collect and hold property taxes and insurance. You will assume this account. (Watch that it is not larger than necessary to cover taxes and insurance when they come due.)

__ *Fire or Casualty:* The contract spells out what happens if the property is damaged prior to closing.

__ *Property Maintenance:* Your contract will require the seller to maintain the property in the same condition it was at the time the contract was signed.

__ *Tenant Leases:* Again, if the property is leased to a tenant, there is a little-used clause that you will want to include. Basically it states: "The seller agrees not to execute new leases or re-lease to existing tenants without prior approval of the buyer." This clause prevents a seller from leasing the home with an undesirable tenant just to collect the income, and prevents a gift to a favorite tenant of a long-term lease. (Both of which you will be stuck with if you buy the home.)

The First Walkthrough Inspection Checklist

General appearance of the property:
- Does the home appear to be well maintained? _____
- Will you need to do extensive painting or repairs? _____
- Is the exterior in good condition, lawn, shrubs, driveway, etc.?_____

Structural Condition:
- Are there signs of dry rot or termite damage? (Wood that is rotted around door frames and the fascia boards near the roof line) _____
- Are there any signs of water leaks? _____ Check ceilings for dark stains.

  Tip: If possible, make your inspection during a rainstorm. Any water damage or leaks will be easily seen.
- Check the exterior walls. Are there any large cracks or signs of severe settling? _____ Minor cracks are normal.
- Are there any areas in the floors that seem to slope or "give" when you walk on them? _____
- Check the basement for signs of water leaks through the exterior walls.

Appliances, Heating and Air Conditioning System, etc.:
- Are all appliances working? _____
- Does the air conditioning and heating system work? _____
- How old are the water heater, heating and air conditioning system? _____
- How old are the appliances and are they in working order? _____

Plumbing:
- Are there any fixtures that leak water or that will not stop running? _____
- Is there any sign of rust or severe corrosion on any of the plumbing fixtures? ____

Is It Livable?
- Is there anything about the home, inside or out, that you just could not live with, at least temporarily? If there is, can it be fixed or replaced at a reasonable cost?

_____

Keep in mind that this is a preliminary walkthrough inspection to determine if there are any obvious reasons you should eliminate this home from your consideration. A complete, formal inspection will be made once you have an agreed-upon offer-to-purchase contract executed. This inspection will examine for everything that can affect the condition and value of the home.

CHAPTER 13

COMMON MISTAKES
BUYERS MAKE AND
HOW TO AVOID THEM

Buying a home will probably be the largest single financial investment you will make in your lifetime. You cannot afford to make any mistakes.

An entire book could be written listing the many ways in which buyers can make mistakes. After reading this chapter, and following its suggestions, you will be able to avoid the most common ones. The comments that follow will also serve as a quick review of the more important points that were made in the buyer section of this book.

SELECTING A HOME

1. **Paying too much for the home.** This can be avoided by doing your homework and knowing what comparable homes are selling for in the neighborhood.

2. **Falling in love with a home you saw . . . especially the first one.** Once this happens, you lose all sense of reasoning (and negotiating power). You have probably done this when buying an automobile. You fall in love with a certain vehicle, buy it anyway you can, as long as you get it, and later wonder why you paid so much for it. On a smaller scale, retailers refer to it as "impulse buying." That's why they put things you really don't need in the most prominent areas of grocery and department stores. If they put them in the

back, once you get to them you decide you've already spent too much money and you pass them by.

The same holds true with home buying. You probably will not get the best possible deal, or maybe not even the most desirable home, if you allow your emotions to control your purchase. There is no question that buying a home is an emotional experience. But you must take the time to look around and to make an informed and negotiated decision too.

3. **Letting the sellers know how much you like their home.** This is a critical mistake that could cost you thousands of dollars or stop you from making the purchase. Once the sellers know you really want their home, you have lost all bargaining power. They may be unwilling to negotiate on the price or any of the other terms you want and need. Your best bet is to act very noncommittal. Let the buyer believe "it's just another home" and you are looking at several before making a final decision.

4. **Buying the most expensive home on the street.** Never make this error. If homes are selling for $150,000 and you pay $200,000, even if your house is worth it, its value will be reduced by the fact that no home on that street is worth it.

5. **Failing to have an inspection made** to uncover any problems with the home.

CONTRACT MISTAKES

1. **Offering too much for a property.** This happens because you did not do your homework. After you read this book, this should not happen. Remember, you can always offer more if your contract is rejected. You can never offer less!

2. **Not saving some areas for negotiation.** It is a good practice to throw a few things into a contract that you don't really need, want, or expect to get. Why? It gives you some bargaining power when negotiating the things you really do want, such as a price concession.

EXAMPLE: You want to buy the home for $165,000 and not the $175,000 being asked. In your contract, you also request that the seller pay for your title insurance policy or that the seller replace the carpet with a better grade that you select. You can, after seeing the home, find several things you'd like to have but which you can do without. Put a few of them in the contract. When the seller looks at the contract, you can, one by one, eliminate the carpet, title insurance payment by the seller or other items you inserted. If the seller comes back with a counter offer on the price (the item you really want to negotiate down) of $173,000, you can say, "I'll tell you what. If you will accept my $165,000 price, I'll cross out the new carpet clause." Each time, you hope to gain a little more on the main concession you want from the seller.

Keep in mind, however, that if you fill your contract full of too many of these requests, the seller may either throw the contract back at you and refuse to negotiate at all, or just cross off every one of them with the first counter offer. Use judgment and put in requests that are not too objectionable, but negotiable. Not all of them should involve the seller paying money.

3. **Not looking over the documents carefully.** If you do not feel comfortable or knowledgeable enough to review the contract or closing documents, hire a professional to do it for you. It is worth the expense.

4. **Not having funds escrowed.** If the seller does not have the agreed-upon repairs made by the day of closing, don't call it off. You have worked long and hard to reach this day. Close on the property and make arrangements with the closing agent to escrow enough of the seller's proceeds to cover the cost of repairs agreed upon but, for whatever the reason, not done. This way you get title to the property at the closing so you can continue with your plans to move in. You probably have the moving van sitting in front of the house waiting for you to arrive with the keys. The seller gets the proceeds from the closing to finance the closing on a new home . . . or take a world cruise, or whatever.

5. **Not making sure you have enough cash to close.** Your closing agent should have furnished you with a statement at least a day or two prior to closing. You need to obtain cashier's checks from your bank in the amount of the funds due at closing. Personal checks are not acceptable and will delay the closing until the checks clear the bank.

Buying a home, especially if it is your first home, can be a frightening experience. You are faced with a situation that is not familiar and you are spending more money at one time than you ever will again. Be assured that it is still a gratifying experience. Once you walk away from the closing and walk through the front door of "Your Home," all your fears will vanish. Mastering the techniques you are learning here will insure that this will be a profitable and non-traumatic experience.

Chapter 14

CLOSING ON
YOUR HOME

You have just purchased your home, but you don't actually own it until you have closed on it. When you are properly prepared for the closing, you will have a better chance of avoiding last-minute problems. You may also be able to save on some of your closing costs. Use the Buyer's Estimated Closing Costs form on page 161 to see how much money you will need.

WHAT THE CLOSING WILL COST

You can expect to pay an average of six percent of the purchase price for closing expenses. You need to understand who collects these fees. We'll assume you are financing the home you are buying. Title insurance is very important, and probably the most expensive cost you will have at the closing: It can be hundreds of dollars, depending on the purchase price of the house. The good news is, it is a one-time cost and it will protect your interests in the event a problem ever occurs with the title to your property while you own it. If it does, you're covered, even after you sell the property and someone in the future finds a problem during the time you owned the property. But, like all insurance policies, you hope you will never collect on it.

TITLE INSURANCE

What exactly is title insurance? When you purchase your home, a title company or attorney examines the chain of titles (previous owners) to insure that there are no problems with obtaining clear title to the property. That chain of title can go back as far as when the United States obtained title to the land from the Indians, Spain, Mexico or whoever had claim to it at that time.

So why do you need title insurance? Let's look at an example. You buy your home from Mr. and Mrs. John Williams. They show up at the closing and both sign the deed over to you. A few months later, you get a call from your attorney telling you there is a problem because Mrs. John Williams just called stating that she understands her husband sold their home. She also states that she does not know who signed the deed as Mrs. John Williams, but it definitely was not her and she still owns the property. Is this a problem? You bet! However, you have title insurance to protect your investment. Without it, you could be out of your home—and of your money.

Now let's carry that example one step further. The real Mrs. John Williams does not show up for ten years. You have since sold the home to someone else. All of a sudden, she shows up to claim her interest. Records show that this all occurred when you bought the home. The problem is still yours, even though you sold the home six years earlier. Again, you'll be glad you have title insurance. It protects you, even after you sell the property, against any problems that may have occurred when you bought it and while you owned it.

The cost of most title insurance policies is based on the cost of the home being insured. There is a sliding scale, which reduces the "per thousand dollars of home value" charge as the cost of the home increases. In other words, the title policy will not generally be a fixed percentage of the entire home cost, but graduate downward as the home value increases.

MORTGAGE FEES

PITI

Included with your monthly mortgage principal and interest payment (the PI portion of the formula) you will also be required to pay an added cost for monthly estimated taxes and insurance (the TI portion of the formula). You probably already know this. Here are some things you may not know:

Escrow Accounts

Most lenders require you pay real estate taxes and insurance on a monthly basis. That cost is added to your monthly mortgage payment. There are a few things to watch out for here.

First, the lender wants to know that there is enough money in your escrow account to pay the real estate tax bill when it comes in. Most tax bills are due on January 1st, but are mailed earlier. You receive a discount if you pay the bill by November 1st or a smaller discount if it is paid by December 1st. The lender will want to pay the bill as soon as it is received. This means you must have the November and December portion of the taxes in your escrow account in advance. Since it is probably already in the escrow account, you will have to buy it from the seller at closing. On the day of closing, you will purchase the escrow account. If the buyer is not assuming the mortgage, the lender will refund the balance in the escrow account, to the seller, minus what is owed up through our example closing date. This is credited to the seller.

Second, we mentioned that the lender wants to have enough money in the escrow account to pay both the tax and insurance bills when they come in. Occasionally, lenders will hold more money than they need. This is your money, sitting in the bank, collecting zero interest, and you can request that the excess be refunded to you.

Third, the opposite situation can also occur. If there is not enough money in the account to pay the tax and/or insurance bills when they come in, you can expect the lender to send you a bill for the deficiency. That could be hundreds of dollars, especially if there has been a sizable tax or insurance increase during the year.

Closing Costs on the Mortgage

Lenders will charge you for quite a few different items. One may be "closing points" which are really a percentage of the loan amount for the purpose of placing the mortgage. These fees are often negotiable. The lender may want to charge you two points to write the mortgage. Two points (2%) on a $125,000 mortgage is $2,500. If mortgage money is easily available, you can probably get this amount reduced or eliminated.

Important Point: Always submit loan applications with two or more lenders. Give yourself a choice and pick the best one. Doing this also gives you negotiating power with some lenders.

Another Important Point: Never forget that banks are a business like any other company. Their business is loaning money at a higher rate of interest than they pay their depositors. Like any other service business, their services are negotiable. They MUST get that money out producing income or the bank will get into financial trouble. Once you understand that the "ivory towers" of a bank house normal business people, trying to sell a service at a profit, you will lose the fear of walking up to a loan officer and saying, "I want to finance a home, but we need to discuss your closing points. ABC bank will loan me the money at the same rate as you and not charge any points. What can we work out?" The worst that can happen is that this bank will stick to its guns and you will go to ABC bank to get your loan.

Other Fees

There are other, more minor, fees that you will incur at the closing. Such costs will include recording of the deed at the county courthouse. (This is how you can prove you own the home.)

There will be charges for various state, county and city taxes and the fee of the attorney or title company who handles your closing.

HINT: If your closing agent also writes the title insurance policy, you may be able to negotiate a much lower fee for closing the transaction. They are also collecting a fee for writing the title policy.

Taxes and Insurance

When we discussed the escrow account you will buy, we mentioned that you will owe the seller for any pre-paid portion of the homeowner insurance plus any pre-paid real estate taxes.

If you are not assuming the seller's homeowner's policy, you will have to purchase your own. Title will not be transferred until you can prove you have the home covered by insurance.

Mortgage Insurance

Mortgage insurance was mentioned earlier as a possible cost, if you have more than an eighty percent mortgage on the home.

Utilities

Water and electric meters will be read on the day of closing and the seller will owe for the utility usage up until that day. You may receive a credit from the seller, if the utility company has a practice of sending a full month's bill at the end of the month. You will also need to make deposits with both the water and electric companies.

Important Point: Be sure to make these deposits prior to closing in order to avoid any interruption in utility services.

Service Contracts

If you are assuming any service contracts currently in force by the seller, you will owe the seller for the unused portion of those contracts that have been pre-paid. These could include pest control, pool and/or lawn services, home maintenance contracts, etc.

SAVING MONEY ON CLOSING COSTS

Here are ways you can save money on your closing costs.

SAVING MONEY ON TITLE INSURANCE

When you buy a title policy to protect your interests, the lender wants a second title policy to protect its interest as well. You know who is going to pay for the lender's title policy, don't you? It sure won't be the lender. You are the one who wants the mortgage. If you didn't know any better, you would be buying your title policy that would cost several hundred dollars plus the lender's policy for an additional several hundred dollars. (The lender's policy charge is usually included in the long list of loan origination fees charged to place the loan.) Your title policy is for the entire amount of the purchase price. The lender's policy will cover only the amount of its mortgage. But that's still quite a bit of money out of your pocket.

Important Point: Request a "simultaneous issue" policy with the lender. You will pay full price for your policy and a second policy will be written to the lender, to cover the amount of the loan, at the same time. This should result in your paying a very small fee for the second policy instead of several hundred dollars. You may have to fight for this because the same party must write both policies. Both your attorney and the lender's attorneys want to write the policy and collect the fees. You may have to use one or the other to handle the entire closing. Most lenders have their own "in house" attorneys on staff and can probably handle your closing for you. If the lender needs to get funds out (mortgages), it may consider letting your attorney write the title policy to cover its mortgage. In that case, your attorney or title company can handle the closing for you and still work a simultaneous issue of both policies.

Negotiable Fees

Don't be afraid to negotiate with anyone who is charging a fee for services. This includes title companies, attorneys, and lenders. Their charges are not set in stone and quite often you can get them to reduce their fees.

Here are some ways you can save money on your home purchase.

1. Getting a new mortgage? Select the lender that will offer you the best terms. State clearly that you are comparing rates and costs and ABC Company is not charging any closing points. If that lender wants to make a loan, which is what it does, it will offer to eliminate these fees.

2. Get the seller to contribute to some of your closing costs. Put yourself in the seller's shoes. Here is a ready, willing, and able buyer on a contract or ready to sign a contract but who wants the seller to pick up the cost of title insurance. The seller has the choice of agreeing to the request, offering to split the cost, or facing the possibility of beginning to market the home all over again. Chances are good that the seller does not want to go back to the beginning and start the marketing process again.

3. If you are buying a new home that is still under construction, you can often negotiate a lower price with the builder if you are handy and agree to do some of the work yourself, such as painting or finishing work.

4. Get the seller to carry the financing. (This subject is covered in detail in another chapter.) You can save a lot of money in closing costs if the seller is willing to carry the mortgage.

5. When you are assuming an existing mortgage, watch the escrow account you are taking over. Quite often there is more money in that account than there needs to be to cover the tax and insurance bills when they must be paid. Request that the excess funds be refunded (probably to the seller). Otherwise, you will be forced to buy out the entire account balance at closing, paying the seller for any portion in the account above what the seller owes up until the day of closing.

6. Check your closing statement carefully. Have each item explained to you by your closing agent. Ask for an explanation of any items you do not understand or agree with. Errors do occur on closing statements that could cost you some money unnecessarily.

THE WALKTHROUGH

In an earlier chapter we discussed that you will have two walkthrough inspections of the home you are buying. The first one takes place at the time you execute a purchase contract. You are now ready to attend the closing so you and the seller make a second walkthrough inspection of the home, prior to closing. You want to insure that everything is the same as it was when you entered into the purchase contract—the home is clean, agreed-to repairs have been completed, and nothing is missing that was supposed to be there. Once you are satisfied, you are ready to attend the closing.

WHAT TO BRING TO THE CLOSING

A day or two before, your closing agent should have supplied you with a statement showing how much money you need to bring to the closing. If all goes well, that check should be all you need to take.

Important Point: Your check must be a bank cashier's check. Personal checks are not acceptable.

HANDLING UNEXPECTED PROBLEMS

Even when you're well prepared, there may be problems that crop up at the closing. Here are a few of the most common ones.

ERRORS IN THE CLOSING STATEMENT

You attend the closing, ready with a cashier's check in hand. Suddenly you discover that there is an error on the closing statement, and it is not in your favor. You need an additional $250 to close. What do you do now? Generally, the closing agent will accept a personal check for the difference.

Why should there be a discrepancy in the amount due? There could be several reasons. The usual one is that the closing was delayed a day or two, which makes all of the prorated figures incorrect.

Perhaps the remaining balance on the mortgage you are assuming is less than the bank originally quoted. This could happen if an additional mortgage payment was made after the bank gave the closing agent a payoff amount. The remaining balance due is now less than you expected.

For example, suppose your closing statement was prepared for an April 5th closing. Your closing agent obtained the final payoff on the mortgage based on closing April 5th. That amount was $42,500. The seller, however, made the April mortgage payment after the payoff balance was given to the closing agent. This means that the mortgage balance is now less than what the buyer was expecting. Depending upon how old the mortgage is, quite a sizable sum of money could be going to the principal reduction of that mortgage. Suppose the actual balance, after the April payment was made, is $42,300. What can the buyer do? The obvious answer is to pay the additional amount in cash at closing. If it is just a couple of hundred dollars, chances are there will not be a problem.

But, what happens if the lender made a mistake and the remaining balance on the mortgage is $5,000 less than the buyer expected? Chances are good that the buyer wll not want to pay or have the money to pay that much more down on the property. One solution is to get the seller to carry a short-term second mortgage for that $5,000. It is in his best interest to do so. If not, he is forced to put the property back on the market and begin the marketing efforts over again. Since the lender is the one who made the mistake, they may be willing to increase the mortgage by $5,000.

A delay in closing can often result in added costs to a buyer or less cash in the pocket of the seller. All prorations must be recalculated when the closing is delayed, and that means the money due at the closing will also change, not just the mortgage balance but the amount of insurance payments and taxes that are escrowed that must also be refigured.

These are not usually insurmountable problems. The buyer and seller can usually come to an agreement to keep the transaction on track.

Buyer's Estimated Closing Costs

ITEM	CHARGE BUYER	CREDIT BUYER
Sales Price	_____	
Earnest Money Deposit		_____
1st Mortgage Amount		_____
2nd Mortgage Amount		_____
New 1st Mortgage Costs	_____	
New 2nd Mortgage Costs	_____	
Appraisal Fee	_____	
Real Estate Taxes paid in advance	_____	
Credit Report	_____	
Settlement Fees (Attorney)	_____	
Title Insurance Cost	_____	

ITEM	CHARGE BUYER	CREDIT BUYER
Document Preparation Fee	_____	
Recording Fees		
Inspection Fees (roof, termite, etc.)		
Survey	_____	
Homeowner Insurance	_____	
Mortgage Insurance	_____	
Other _____	_____	
Total Charges (Include Sale Price)		_____
Total Credits		_____
Estimated Cash Due at Closing (Total Charges – Total Credits)		_____
Totals (Both columns should add up to the same amount)	_____	_____

NOTE: The above figures are for estimated purposes only. A formal closing statement will be prepared by the closing agent and given to the buyer, for review, prior to closing.

Some of the charges shown may not be applicable in a given area. Others may be added that are not included here. Check with your attorney or closing agent.

In most areas you can expect buyer closing costs to average about 6% of the selling price.

CHAPTER 15

WHAT YOU NEED TO KNOW ABOUT MORTGAGES AND FINANCING REAL ESTATE

Financing can be a critical part of your home purchase. Unfortunately, many buyers venture a home purchase, especially if it is their first one, blindly looking for any mortgage they can obtain. On the next few pages, we will explore the ins and outs of mortgage financing, how lenders operate, where to find mortgages, and, finally, how to get the best possible mortgage.

The first fact you need to understand and believe is that banks and savings and loan associations are all businesses, just like your business or the company for whom you work, that want to make money. The only difference is that they are in the business of collecting money from depositors and lending it out at a higher rate of interest than they are paying their depositors for the use of their money. We are often afraid to discuss our financing needs with them. We'll accept anything they are willing to give us and bend over backwards to make them happy. This point is discussed in both the buyer and seller sections of this book.

APPLYING FOR A MORTGAGE

Now let's look at the real world of lenders. As we mentioned, they are business people. They want to make money. The more depositors they have and are paying interest to, the more loans they need to make in order to pay this interest. What does this mean to you? When you are looking for a mortgage on the home you want to buy, you need to do the following:

1. Submit your loan application to at least two or more lenders.

2. Sit down with the loan officers and discuss *your* needs, not theirs. Tell them what you need and ask how they can help you. Now, let's face it, if you walk into your bank with a track record of huge debt, late payments and a recent bankruptcy, no one may be too willing to talk with you. If, however, you are an average individual you will have no problem.

3. When you discuss financing of a home, keep in mind that, although your credit record will be important, this is not the only factor considered in making a loan. In large part the fair market value of the home you want financed will determine how much money will be lent. A multiplier will be applied to the value and a loan percentage worked out based on that figure. In other words, if your home appraises at $175,000, a lender may be willing to loan ninety or ninety-five percent of that amount. The basis will be not only on your credit, but the amount of equity (security) you have in the home once the loan is placed.

4. Since you have submitted loan applications to two or more lenders, you can pick the one that is offering the best terms and conditions.

5. You can even suggest to one lender that ABC Bank is willing to give you this or that. Can it compete?

As we progress through this chapter, you will learn all kinds of techniques for obtaining the best possible financing. You'll also learn where to locate a mortgage other than from a bank.

HOW A MORTGAGE WORKS

There are two parts to a mortgage: the mortgage itself and the note. The mortgage spells out the terms and conditions; the note is the personal note you execute guaranteeing the lender that you will pay back the mortgage under the specified terms and conditions spelled out in the mortgage. Both documents will be recorded in the courthouse public records in the county in which the property is located.

You already know that when you make a mortgage payment, a portion goes to the reduction of the principal or remaining balance due on the mortgage, and a portion goes toward payment of interest you pay to the lender for the use of the money. (Remember, that's how lenders make enough money to pay their depositors. While they may pay them 4 or 5% interest, they will charge you 7 or 8%.)

Your mortgage will probably include an additional amount to cover the escrowing of funds to pay taxes and insurance when the bills come in. (The lender wants to insure that its investment is secure and those bills are paid.)

You already know that most of the mortgage payment you make, especially in the early years, is almost entirely all interest payment and very little principal reduction. Here is an example of a first year of mortgage payments on a $100,000 mortgage amortized over 30 years at 7 percent interest.

Monthly mortgage payments will be $665.30 or $7,983.60 a year. Of that amount, $1,015.78 will be reduction of your $100,000. The remaining $6,967.82 is interest payment. Each succeeding year, however, more of your payment will go toward principal reduction.

How to Save Money
with Short-Term Mortgages

You have no doubt heard the commercials promoting the short-term mortgage and how much money you can save in interest payments over the life of the mortgage by reducing the payoff term. No doubt you will save considerable interest by doing so, but there is also a down side.

Suppose you decide to amortize the above mortgage over a fifteen-year term rather than a thirty-year term. Over the life of the thirty-year mortgage, you will pay the lender $139,508.90 in interest. If, however, you pay off that mortgage in only fifteen years, you will pay $61,789.09 in interest. That is a savings to you of $77,719.81. Sound good? What you need to consider is that your mortgage payments will increase considerably in order to pay the mortgage back in half the time. Monthly mortgage payments on a fifteen-year loan will be $898.83. That is a $233.53-a-month increase over a thirty-year mortgage. This idea is great if you can comfortably pay the added monthly mortgage payments.

There is another solution. If you amortize a mortgage over thirty years (to keep the monthly payment down) and make an extra payment every so often, you will still greatly reduce the overall term of the mortgage. The nice part is, you are not obligated to make that extra payment if money is tight. If you make one, which, by the way, does not have to be a normal size mortgage payment, make sure you do it by separate check and mark the check "toward principal balance on the mortgage." You don't want the bank to think you are making an extra full principal and interest payment during the month, or it will apply most of it to interest and not to principal reduction. There is a good chance that, if it is considered an extra full payment, the lender will still expect the normal payment the first of the next month.

PREPAYING MONTHLY MORTGAGE PAYMENTS

On the other side of the coin, suppose you are a schoolteacher and are paid three months' salary at the beginning of the summer vacation period since school will not be in session. A friend of mine thought it made sense to make three mortgage payments in the month of June to insure that the extra money did not "disappear" before the July and August mortgage payments became due. She sent the lender a check to cover all three months' payments. The lender proceeded to give her credit for one month principal and interest payment and apply the remaining two payments to principal reduction. The big shock came on July 1st when she was informed that the July mortgage payment was now due, when she had already paid the bank all the money she had available.

How do you avoid the problem? The sure way is to put that extra money aside, where you won't be tempted to spend it on something else, and make normal monthly mortgage payments when they come due. If you just cannot resist the temptation to blow it on a trip to Florida, do the next best thing. Sit down with a lender and explain that you want to make the June, July and August payments now and be sure your mortgage account is credited as such. You may be safer if you write three separate checks and clearly identify each: For June Payment, For July Payment and For August Payment.

Important Point: That identification should be written into the top of the "endorsement" area on the back of the check. If the bank still fouls up and credits them all in the same month, you have the cancelled checks to prove that you specified how those payments were to be credited. Writing it in the endorsement area serves two purposes. First, it will be difficult for the check processor to miss it. Second, and probably just as important, you should have no problem proving the statement was on the check when it was received. If you put it on the "remarks" section at the bottom of the face of the check, the lender can always say that you added it when the check came back after being deposited by the bank. This is not to suggest that banks may be dishonest. It's just that in today's automated computer society, many details are overlooked when humans do not do the work. Fortunately, most checks are credited manually because the amount of the check has to be typed into the computer system.

HOW PRINCIPAL AND INTEREST PAYMENTS ARE CALCULATED

Here is a bit of information you will probably never need, but you may be interested in knowing how mortgage payments are figured. Here is the four-step process using the above 15-year, $100,000 mortgage at 7% interest with monthly payments of $898.83:

1. Multiply the mortgage amount ($100,000) times the annual interest rate (7% or .07). That's $7,000. Divide that amount by 12 months. 7,000/12 = $583.33. This figure represents the first month's interest payment.

2. Subtract the $583.33 from the monthly mortgage payment of $898.83 and you have the amount the principal balance is reduced the first month. ($898.83 – $583.33 = $315.50)

3. To determine the remaining balance on the mortgage, subtract the $315.50 principal payment from the beginning loan balance of $100,000. ($100,000 – $315.50 = $99,684.50) The remaining balance on the mortgage after the first payment is $99,684.50.

4. Follow the above three steps to determine the breakdown of principal and interest for the second month, only use the new mortgage balance at the end of the first month, $99,684.50.

This process must be repeated each month for the entire fifteen-year period, 180 payments. Now you know why they invented financial calculators and mortgage amortization schedules.

MORTGAGE INSURANCE

If your mortgage is large and your equity is small, the lender will no doubt require you to pay for a mortgage insurance policy. This protects its interest in case you can no longer meet mortgage payments. Unfortunately, the bank is usually the sole beneficiary to the policy and the monthly charge increases your mortgage payment.

Important Point: Once you can prove that you have twenty percent equity in the home, the lender should be willing to eliminate the requirement for mortgage insurance. Ask!

TYPES OF MORTGAGES

On the next few pages we will look at various options that may be open to you when you finance your home. Not all mortgages or lenders are the same. You will discover some alternate ways you may consider when looking for a home mortgage. You will also learn the cautions you need to observe if certain types of mortgages are offered to you.

Variable Rate Mortgages

Although they are not too prevalent in today's residential mortgage market, variable rate mortgages are still used. They will fluctuate with the current market conditions. The lender is generally relying on interest rates increasing and this affords the opportunity of increasing your interest rate accordingly.

Important Point: If you do agree to a variable rate mortgage, make sure there is a cap or limit on how much the lender can increase it in any one year, and a cap on the maximum amount the rate can be increased over the term of the loan.

Graduated Payment Mortgages

A graduated payment mortgage, if available, is a way of keeping your payment down during the first years of the loan and gradually increasing them as your ability to pay increases. If current interest rates are 7%, you may start out with payments based on 5% interest and each year or so that rate will increase, thereby increasing your monthly payments. You will probably pay an above-current interest rate for most of the life of the loan, but it is a way to get into home ownership when you are just getting started.

Reverse Equity Mortgages

Reverse equity mortgages have become popular in recent years. They appeal primarily to retired homeowners, who have their home paid off and could use extra income on which to live. Each month, the bank sends the homeowner a check, which, of course, adds to the remaining balance due on the mortgage. Caution must be used in accepting this type of loan, although it could end up less expensive than borrowing money if you need it. Most reverse equity mortgages are written so the homeowner(s) can continue using that money the remainder of their lives. When they die, the bank will generally take over the property. It's not a profitable solution for the heirs, but it insures the elderly homeowner(s) the security of having a home in which to live.

Balloon Mortgages

Many mortgages are written with a "balloon" payment due at the end of a certain number of years. In our earlier example, the $100,000 mortgage may be written for a 30-year term, but balloon in 15 years. Properly used, it can be a welcome financing technique and not one to be avoided at all costs. The advantage is that you are able to amortize the loan over 30 years, thus keeping the monthly payments down ($665.30 instead of $898.83 on the 15-year mortgage). So what do you do at the end of 15 years when the $74,020 remaining balance is due and payable?

First of all, do you think you will still own the home fifteen years from now? Most people move about every seven years. If you sell it, the loan will be paid off by the buyer. If you do still own the home, you will merely renegotiate it with the present lender or apply for a new loan through someone else. By that time, you will have considerably more equity in the home than when you first financed it, so obtaining a new mortgage should not be a problem.

*A **word of caution:*** When agreeing to a balloon mortgage, make sure you keep the balloon term as long as possible. Avoid short-term balloons where the balance is due in a year or two, unless you expect your rich uncle to die in the next twelve months and you are his sole beneficiary.

Important Point: If you do have a balloon mortgage, do not wait until just before the balloon is due before you start looking for a new mortgage. You can even start looking a year or two before the balloon comes due if the mortgage market is good at that time.

Deferred Payment Mortgages

There are times when you may be able to ask the lender to defer mortgage payments for a short period of time, if you have a good reason. This is especially true if you are taking over a distressed property and want the lender to defer payments so you can use that money to renovate the home. Normally the loan period will just be extended for that period of time plus interest added. Instead of a 25-year mortgage, you may end up with a 25-1/2-year mortgage. So what? You won't be living in that home twenty-five years from now anyway. The only thing it does do is cost you additional interest over the term of the loan.

WRAPAROUND MORTGAGE

Wraparound mortgages, sometimes called All Inclusive Deeds of Trust, can often solve a financing problem when you want a reluctant seller to carry a second mortgage. Here is how it works. Suppose the lender is only willing to give you a $50,000 mortgage, or there is a desirable $50,000 mortgage already on the property that you would like to assume. Unfortunately, you need $75,000 in financing to buy the home. The seller refuses to carry the $25,000 added mortgage you need to make the deal. You suggest preparing a wraparound mortgage in the amount of $75,000 to cover both the existing first mortgage and the seller second.

Here is how it works: The seller will carry a $75,000 wraparound mortgage. You agree to pay 8% interest on the mortgage. The lender's mortgage, which is being assumed, is a nice low 6.5% loan. (That's why you wanted to assume it.) Why will the seller go along with this program? Theoretically, the seller is still carrying a second mortgage because the primary lender is still in first place. What does the seller gain? The seller will be collecting 8% interest on a $75,000 mortgage, even though only $25,000 is invested in the total loan. In other words, the seller will earn 8% on a $25,000 investment plus a 1.5% override on the lender's $50,000 mortgage. That 1.5% can average an additional $750 a year in profit without anyone doing anything. **A word of caution, however:** Lenders may not like knowing the property is that heavily financed, if it is discovered.

Important Point: It is generally accepted practice, under a wraparound mortgage, that the seller (mortgagee) will collect the entire mortgage payment and be responsible for continuing to pay the existing first mortgage. This is not a good idea, since you may not know if the seller is making timely payments to the bank, until you get a notice that the first mortgage is in default. If you consider using the wraparound mortgage approach, you need to have a third, impartial party collect the entire monthly payment and disburse the proper amounts to the bank and to the seller. Bank trust departments may handle it for a modest fee. (You may not want to use the bank that is holding the primary mortgage if it has indicated any displeasure about wraparound mortgages.)

FHA AND VA FINANCING

Some available loans are guaranteed by the federal government. The FHA or Federal Housing Administration is one such agency. It makes qualifying for a mortgage easier than if you had to rely on the lender's policy alone. If you are a veteran (and that includes being in the military service at virtually any time), you may qualify for a VA loan which often offers very favorable rates and extremely low down-payment mortgages. These mortgages also involve more "red tape" than a conventional loan, but you may find it worthwhile to check into it.

If you are interested in either of these types of mortgages, contact your lender or mortgage broker for current information and qualification requirements.

SELLER FINANCING

When working on the financing of a home, always ask if the seller will consider carrying a mortgage. This is the ideal solution. You can generally negotiate a better interest rate and avoid many of the normal closing costs of a new mortgage.

SECOND MORTGAGES

Here are a few more facts you should know about second mortgages:

1. As far as you are concerned, it should not matter how many mortgages are on a property as long as the total amount of the mortgages is what you want and the average interest rate and payment amount are satisfactory. Having the mortgage broken up into two different ones gives you the flexibility to pay off the second mortgage without disturbing the first. When trying to reduce your overall debt, this is an easy way

to make a lump-sum mortgage payment and reduce your monthly payments. Making a large payment on a first mortgage will reduce the remaining balance but probably will not reduce your monthly payments. It will just be paid off over a fewer number of years.

2. Banks do not like to know you have a second mortgage on the property, even though they are still in first position. Getting a second mortgage reduces your equity and increases the bank's risk. As a practical matter, chances are the first mortgage holder will never know that you added a second mortgage through a private lender. This explains why so many loan companies are thriving on loaning money on the equity you have in your home. Some will even loan 110% of the property's value.

Here is how to determine if a second mortgage makes financial sense. It's called Interest Averaging.

INTEREST AVERAGING

An easy way to select the best alternative is interest averaging. Suppose you are still looking for that $100,000 mortgage we discussed earlier. There is a $75,000 assumable first mortgage on the property at 7%. You want the seller to carry a second mortgage, but she wants 12% interest on the $25,000 she would have to hold. Your first reaction may be "Forget it. I can get a new mortgage for the full $75,000 at only 9%." This is where interest averaging comes into the picture. Here is an easy way to determine which financing alternative is the best for you. The first is a new $100,000 mortgage at 9% interest. Multiply $100,000 × .09 or 9% and the result is $9,000. Now let's look at the second alternative. Assume the existing mortgage, $75,000, at 7% interest: $75,000 × .07 or 7% = $5,250.

The seller second mortgage is $25,000 × 12% interest or $25,000 × .12 = 3,000.

Now add the two together: $5,250 + $3,000 and the result is $8,250, or $750 a year less than the new first mortgage. In spite of the high 12% seller mortgage, you will still be paying less interest per year.

Not all financing alternatives work out this well. Sometimes they won't work out at all, but you now know an easy way to figure out the best alternative.

WHEN TO CONSIDER A LEASE/OPTION

You've done your homework, checked with several lenders and looked over your budget. No matter how much you want to buy a home, you just don't qualify. Are you doomed to renting? Not necessarily. If you have found a home you like, *and a seller who is motivated to sell,* try a lease-option. Here is how it works:

You approach the seller to say that you would like to buy the home, but right now, you just can't swing it. Since the seller wants to get out from under that home, you are willing to rent it, with an option to purchase it within the next three years. You enter into a formal lease/option contract, spelling out the terms and conditions of the lease and option to purchase. You agree on a monthly rent, who pays for what as far as utilities, taxes, insurance, repairs, etc. You also negotiate on a price at which you can buy the home, if you choose to do so.

One more point to be negotiated is the down payment. You request that a specified part, like one-half, of each month's rent be applied toward a down payment. Once you have sufficient "credit equity" to purchase the home, you do so.

Important Point: Option contracts, like purchase contracts, must have a time limit for a "closing." In the case of the option contract, both the buyer and seller must agree on when the buyer will have sufficient equity to close on the sale. The seller may not want the option contract to run for several years and still not know if the home is really sold.

RISKS TO YOU

The seller may request some type of option money up front, in case you default on the monthly rent or decide not to buy the home. That option money will be lost if you walk away from the deal.

After living in the home for a year or more, you may decide you really don't like the house, the neighborhood or the neighbors. You must either continue with the purchase or forfeit your deposit.

If something happens to you during the option period, and you are unable to close, you may still be forced to close on the purchase or lose your option money.

BENEFITS TO YOU

You have the opportunity to move into the home you want without having to qualify for a mortgage. Although you are still paying rent, part of your rent payment is accruing toward your down payment. You have the security of knowing that you are making payments toward your own home purchase.

RISKS TO THE SELLER

The seller still owns the home and is now renting it.

There is no way of knowing if you will eventually close on the purchase. Three years from now, the original owner may still own the home and you will be free to walk away. That is why a time limit must be set for transfer of title to the buyer and you can be expected to put up some nonrefundable option money.

The seller is trusting that you will take care of the home and continue making timely rent payments.

The owner has received no money from the home. This could be a problem if the cash from the present home is needed as a down payment on the new one. You also are getting credit for part of each month's rent.

Needless to say, you must find a very motivated seller to enter into a lease/option contract.

BENEFITS TO THE SELLER

The seller is free to move to the new location.

Chances are good that the rent you pay will exceed mortgage payments and the other agreed-upon expenses so that there will be a little money each month.

One final point needs to be negotiated. Earlier, we stated that you both agree to a selling price and have three years to close. If you are in a seller's market, the seller may not want to commit to a price based on today's market. In three years, the home could be worth considerably more than it is today, but the seller is locked in on a fixed price. A knowledgeable seller will request that the purchase price be adjusted to current market value at the time you are ready to exercise your option and close on the purchase. Conversely, if market conditions are poor, whenever you are ready to close, the home may be worth less than you are expected to pay. Fortunately, if you selected a home in a good neighborhood and agreed to a fair market price for it, the chances of it being worth less are slim.

Although lease/options are not the easiest and best way to get into a home, they do solve a problem when both buyer and seller can agree to the transaction. If all else fails, it may be worth considering.

MORTGAGE CLAUSE CAVEATS

Here is a list of mortgage clauses to watch out for when financing a property or assuming an existing mortgage.

Watch out for prepayment penalties in a mortgage: You may not want to keep paying on a mortgage for the full term. Rather, you may want to pay it off in advance, like when you win the lottery. Some mortgages have clearly-stated penalty clauses written into them. If you pay it off before the normal amortization period, you will have to pay a prepayment penalty. This can also be a problem if you are selling a home and the buyer does not want to assume the existing mortgage. Keep this in mind because you will be a seller someday and may be stuck with a mortgage that cannot be prepaid.

Watch out for balloon payment clauses: If the mortgage has a balloon clause, as we discussed earlier, it must, by law, be written in bold print across the mortgage document that "This Mortgage Has A Balloon Clause" or some similar wording. Do not enter into such a mortgage unless you follow the advice given earlier in this chapter.

Watch out for 110% mortgages: There is another type of home financing that is showing up on the market, primarily through private lending sources, such as local loan companies. They will loan you up to 110% of the value of your home. If you are really desperate for money, it is a source, but you have just eliminated the equity you have in your home plus 10% more than the market value. You need to ask if they are loaning you the money based on the fair market value of the home or on the "appraised" value. The appraised value is usually somewhat less than what the home is really worth. What does this mean to you? You have a home worth $100,000 (if you were to sell it tomorrow). The appraised value, however, is only $80,000 according to the county tax appraiser's office. If that lender is willing to loan you 110% of the appraised value, that's $88,000 or quite a bit less than the fair market value. In any event, be very cautious when overfinancing your home. Not only are you putting yourself at financial risk, but you can also expect this type of loan to carry a high rate of interest.

Watch out for a nonassumable clause: More often than not, mortgages today are not assumable when you want to sell. The mortgage will have to be paid off and a new owner qualify for a new one. If a buyer wants to assume an existing mortgage, it may be at the discretion of the lender as to the terms, conditions and interest rate on the assumption. You need to watch this carefully when you buy. You may think you are assuming a 7% mortgage, but the lender has the right to increase that interest rate on an assumption. It may also be possible to negotiate a new mortgage with the present lender at better rates than securing a new one somewhere else.

Why are most mortgages no longer assumable? In the 1970s, when the mortgage market and economy went through the roof with double-digit inflation, lenders were forced to pay depositors double-digit interest rates on savings deposits. At the same time, they were locked into long-term mortgages at 6% and 8% interest. Remember, lenders need to charge more interest on the loans they make than they pay their depositors. The above situation caused many banks to fail and put those that survived into a loss situation. They don't intend to get into that situation again, so they protect themselves by making sure mortgages are not assumable. They can then renegotiate them at whatever the current rate happens to be.

This again emphasizes the importance of shopping around for a mortgage. Interest rates and available mortgage money vary from day to day and from lender to lender.

USING A MORTGAGE BROKER

There is another alternative to financing that you might want to consider: mortgage brokers. Mortgage brokers are in the business to find you the best mortgage that is available, for which they are paid by you. They have a big advantage over you looking for a mortgage on your own: They are in contact with several lenders and keep track of who has money available at the best rate and terms at any particular time. They can often negotiate a better mortgage than you can because their business is in giving lenders customers and working out the details. (Again, keep in mind that banks are just another business, looking for customers.) You can expect the mortgage broker to charge either a flat fee for successfully placing a mortgage for you, or perhaps a percentage, such as 1% of the amount of the mortgage you obtain. Just remember, you can and should negotiate with most of them.

For more information on mortgages, read Chapter 18, Banks, Mortgage Brokers, and Other Lenders.

PART THREE

WORKING WITH APPRAISERS, INSPECTORS, AND OTHER PROFESSIONALS

Before you complete the sale or purchase of your home, you will no doubt be working with some outside professionals, even if you have planned on doing it all yourself. This section of the book is devoted to the various professionals you may be exposed to and end up working with. You'll learn what each group does and how it does it. Even if you have no need for its services, it is a good idea to know what the purpose is of each group when you buy or sell your home. You may be able to use some of this knowledge on your own.

Here are the various professionals you may need to assist you in selling, buying and closing on a home.

- *Property Appraisers* are a must if you intend to finance your home purchase. The lender will require an appraisal of the home to determine how much money it will be willing to loan you.

- *Home Inspection Services* will certainly be required by a buyer to insure that there are no major problems that need to be addressed prior to closing. In some states, a home inspection is mandatory.

- *Mortgage Brokers, Banks, and Other Lenders:* If you intend to finance the purchase of your home, you will need to be familiar with the various options available to you for locating the best possible mortgage.

- *Realtors* will be contacted only if you decide that it is not worth doing all the work yourself.

- *Title Companies and Attorneys* are a must when you purchase a home to insure that everything is in order and that you receive a clear and marketable title to the home.

It may appear that you need to employ outside services in order to buy or sell a home. To a certain degree, you do. You will, however, be able to eliminate the major expenses you would pay if you had everything done for you. Knowing what is usually done by them will enable you to apply some of these methods and tactics yourself. Perhaps you will not need each of the services, but you will have a better understanding of how they all work, what they do and how they do it

CHAPTER 16

APPRAISERS

Throughout this book we discuss the importance of pricing your home at fair market value, which is the price at which homes comparable to yours are selling. One of the methods used to establish this value is by doing exactly what you can do yourself. You should get a CMA (Comparative Market Analysis).

Appraisers are individuals who are licensed by their state to establish fair market values of the properties they are qualified to appraise.

Some appraisers may use the designation MAI which stands for Member of the Appraisers' Institute. This is a professional designation earned by some appraisers after they have completed advanced degrees in property appraisal. Not only are they licensed by the state to be qualified to appraise property, but have gone one step further to complete additional course studies. (Kind of like getting a Masters degree.)

THE REAL ESTATE BROKER
AS APPRAISER

Most real estate brokers, in accordance with the licensing laws of the state, are allowed to perform appraisals on a property and give a written estimate of market value. There are usually a couple of important restrictions included. They are permitted to appraise only the types of properties in which they work and with which they are familiar. In other words, a broker who lists and sells only office buildings cannot give an appraisal on a home. Second, a broker cannot offer an appraisal on a property that is outside of his or her marketing area. For example, a broker who is actively selling homes in Buffalo, New York would not be knowledgeable about the New York City market, and therefore could not offer a formal appraisal on a home in New York City.

A word of caution: A real estate broker must not appraise a property in which there is personal involvement. In other words, a broker cannot (or ethically should not) give a formal, written appraisal if he or she is listing the property. That is a conflict of interest. However, do not confuse a formal appraisal with a CMA. There is nothing wrong with a broker preparing a CMA in order to establish the fair market value of a property for listing purposes. A CMA does not reflect the value judgment of the broker but rather an analysis of what has sold and already closed. But if the broker is considering buying the property personally, there could be a question of conflict of interest. It is possible to include only the "prior sales" in the report that benefit the broker (or the buyer or seller for that matter). How? The individual obtaining a CMA can leave out the higher- or lower-priced comparables, depending on its purpose. If you are selling a home, you may be tempted to eliminate any comparable homes in your area that sold for less than you want the CMA report to show. Conversely, if you prepare a CMA as a buyer, you may be tempted to delete the higher-priced homes that have sold to show the seller that the price is too high. Use of either tactic, especially by a broker, is highly unethical. Keep in mind that either party can run the same CMA and recognize that the information you furnished is not accurate. It could destroy your chance of negotiating a sale or purchase of that home.

WHY YOU NEED AN APPRAISAL

First of all, let's look at the two primary reasons for getting an appraisal on a property you intend to sell or want to buy. You, as a buyer or seller, want to get a "ballpark" figure of what your home is worth on today's market. That's where the CMA (Comparative Market Analysis) comes in. Most appraisers agree that it is the best method for establishing the market value of a property.

There is a second reason for an appraisal. It is required for a lender, in order to determine the market value of a property for loan or mortgage purposes. Most lenders have their own in-house appraisers. So you may see a different value put on your home than that arrived at by your own independent, outside appraiser. Why?

First of all, the lender is usually cautious when it comes to keeping its loans secure. Your home may have a market value of $150,000, but the lender may receive a valuation of $135,000 from its in-house appraiser. This provides a $15,000 cushion for market changes or errors in the estimate. The lender will then use a formula to determine what percentage of that $135,000 it feels safe in lending. Keep in mind: The lender cannot afford to make a huge financial mistake with its depositors' money. If it does, it comes out of the lender's pocket. You may be looking for a 90% mortgage, but it will loan only 90% of $135,000, not $150,000. It also frequently uses another multiplier that further reduces that $135,000 even more before applying the 90% mortgage allowance. This can be a shock to a home buyer who is looking for a 90% mortgage on the purchase price of $150,000 ($135,000) and receives instead a 90% loan of only $121,500. This means somehow an additional $13,500 must be obtained in order to close.

HOW PROPERTIES ARE APPRAISED

There are three basic methods for conducting a property appraisal: the comparable value approach, the replacement cost method, and the income approach to value.

THE COMPARABLE VALUE APPROACH

The appraiser researches comparable sales (comps) in the area. "Comparable" means several things.

First, the appraiser must look up sold properties that are in the same area as the subject property. Those sales should ideally have been completed within the previous twelve months. This may not always be an easy task in a neighborhood where there have been relatively few homes sold, and the research may have to go back further than just twelve months. Of course the further back the appraiser must look for solds, the less accurate they are. Quite often, past sales values must be adjusted to reflect the current market.

Next, the properties being used as comparables should closely match the one being appraised. This narrows the comparable list even further. Obviously, if you are selling a four-bedroom home on a 150 × 200-foot lot, you cannot compare that home with a two-bedroom home on a 75 × 200-foot lot, even if they are next door to each other. The appraisal must be modified to compensate for the differences between the comps and the subject property.

Once a list of comparable sales has been compiled and adjusted as needed in order to make them truly comparable, the appraiser comes up with an average value of the homes that have been sold.

The Replacement Cost Method

This is exactly what the term implies. The appraiser estimates what it would cost to duplicate the present home on an identical lot today. There are some problems with this method. First of all, chances are good that there are no identical or even comparable vacant lots in that immediate area to use for valuation purposes.

How is that resolved? The appraiser researches, as best as possible, what the most recent sales of vacant lots in the area have been. Then their selling prices must be adjusted based on how much the market has changed. At times all that is possible is a fair market estimate of what that lot would sell for today, if it were available.

Once the market value of that lot is established, next the cost of duplicating the home on the lot must be calculated. This requires several steps. The first one is to determine what building costs are running per square foot of livable floor space, again using the same type of construction as the home being appraised. The home will be measured to determine the replacement cost. Next, consideration will be made for the part of the home that is not under air conditioning and heating. The replacement cost of that portion will be less. Garages, for example, are usually basic structures with no air conditioning or heat and basic drywall finishing. The roof may not even be insulated. The cost of building that portion, on a price-per-square-foot basis, will be less than the finished home. Now there is a total price for replacing the basic home, but in a stripped condition. Kitchens and bathrooms cost more to build than bedrooms. The appraiser usually estimates a higher per-square-foot cost to these rooms to cover the cost of appliances, sinks and plumbing.

If the home has special features, such as a bay window, French doors, extra-quality carpeting or floor tiles, wall treatments, etc., more may be added for these features. The total reflects the cost of a duplicate home. But these estimates are based on a NEW home, while this one may be fifteen years old. The next job is to reduce the new home cost by a percentage, depending on the age of the subject property.

Finally, the appraiser adds the value of exterior improvements, shrubs, driveways, fences, etc. All of this information is compiled to produce the final estimated market value of the home.

In simple form, the appraisal may look like this:

Land Value		=	$ 40,000
Basic Home—$40 Sq. Ft., × 2000 Sq. Ft. = $80,000			
Less 10% adjustment for age =	8,000	=	72,000
Additional Improvements		=	20,000
Exterior Improvements		=	15,000
Total Estimate of Market Value			$147,000

THE INCOME APPROACH TO VALUE METHOD

This method of property appraisal is used primarily on income-producing investment properties and is based on its income or profit potential. (For real estate investors, this is the most meaningful method of appraising a property.)

There are three different formulas used for a complete investment property estimate of market value. The first two mentioned above are used, but with a twist. An apartment building's value may be estimated using the comparable method by figuring a one-bedroom apartment is worth $35,000 and a two-bedroom unit is worth $45,000. This method is probably the least accurate method and the appraiser will usually give it the least weight when compiling the three estimates.

The appraiser uses the three estimates to determine a market value of the investment property. The result is not an average. Get an estimate giving the most value to the CMA or actual properties sold rather than a replacement cost.

In the case of income-producing property, the income approach to market value is the most accurate method of estimating market value.

CHAPTER 17

HOME INSPECTORS

Home inspections are a must when a home is being sold. The buyer is certain to request one to make sure the home has no termites, the roof does not leak, all of the appliances and HVAC system are in working order, etc. (HVAC stands for Heating, Ventilating, and Air Conditioning.) Some states' laws may require home inspections be made prior to the sale of a property.

Who does home inspections? Most cities have several companies that specialize in making a comprehensive examination of the home and preparing a lengthy report of findings and what they checked. The buyer will pay to have the inspection done, unless negotiated otherwise. The buyer is the one who wants the inspection and it's the buyer who wants to be certain that the inspector is impartial.

SELECTING AN INSPECTOR

Check out a home inspector carefully; make sure the one you choose is licensed, at least by the city and perhaps also by the state. Most states require home inspectors to be licensed and have varying degrees of education that qualifies them to conduct inspections and prepare a formal opinion of the condition of the house.

You will find several home inspection companies listed in the Yellow Pages. If you randomly call any of them, request as much information as you can get. How long have they been in business? What are their qualifications? How many home inspections have they done? Request details on what type of presentation they prepare and what they charge for their services. Carefully screen each potential applicant. You

187

may also contact people you know who have had an inspection done and find out who they used and if they were satisfied with the professionalism of the home inspector.

CAUTION: Real estate brokers often suggest a home inspector that they use. If you use a broker, make sure the suggested inspector is impartial and not willing to overlook some of the necessary inspections in order to insure that the broker's sale will close.

Conversely, as the seller of the property, you do not want a home inspector who will find ten pages of faults with your home. Even though most of them may be small or easy to fix (a leaking water faucet, for example), you don't want to have the buyer facing a huge report of everything that is wrong with your home. A lengthy list of defects, no matter how small they may be, can give the buyer second thoughts about the condition of the home.

THE HOME INSPECTION REPORT

Here are the basic details that will be found in a home or condominium inspection report and the various inspections that will be made.

The basic report may consist of several different parts:

1. Title Page—Information about the home being inspected: Location, age, size, etc.

2. Property Inspection Report—(Details below)

3. Summary Page—Deficiencies found and estimated cost to resolve them

4. Information about the company making the inspection

5. The scope of the inspection to be made

6. Procedures to be followed for the inspection

A sample inspection report is included at the end of this chapter, beginning on page 190. The inspection company may also include one or more pages of explanation about how the inspection was conducted and what items were or were not included and why. The report may also include the qualifications of the company.

Building inspection reports are quite comprehensive. Your main concerns in any inspection are the big-ticket items: termites, roof, heating and air conditioning system, appliances and water heater. There might be many "little" things wrong, but most of them will be easily and inexpensively fixed. This is the reason we suggest you, as a seller, may want to have a preliminary inspection made in order to take care of these minor and some major problems before the buyer has an inspection made.

There is another advantage in knowing what deficiencies may be found in your home before a buyer does. You can have them repaired, often less expensively than the buyer may want you to spend for them.

As an example, you know there is a slight roof leak in one corner of the home. Having a roofer replace the tarpaper and shingles in that one corner is a minor cost and will solve the problem. If, however, the buyer's inspector detects that same leak, the buyer may insist that the entire roof be replaced. After all, it will be at the seller's expense.

As a practical matter, even if your home is not sold, a leaking roof needs to be repaired before it becomes a major problem. You should want to know about it now.

At first look, home inspectors may seem like a good way to kill a sale, by finding so many faults with a home that the buyer will walk away from the contract. This is the reason for having a "repair" clause in the contract. You agree to pay for up to "X" number of dollars or a certain percentage of the selling price to cover the cost of needed repairs. If something shows up that is a serious problem and exceeds the agreed-upon amount for repairs, the buyer and seller can always negotiate a revised price.

One final point: If your contract allows for up to 2% of the purchase price for repairs ($3,000 on a $150,000 purchase price), you can surely expect the buyer to find every way possible to get that entire $3,000.

Sample Home Inspection Report

1. **Termite Inspection: (Wood-destroying organisms)**
   - Visible evidence of wood-destroying organisms
   - Live wood-destroying organisms
   - Visible damage from wood-destroying organisms
   - Treatment required
   - Both subterranean and structural termite inspections are done
   - Generally, according to your state law, termite inspections are good for 30 days

2. **Radon Gas:** An invisible and odorless gas that is present in the soil in some areas of the country. The test is a simple canister left in the home for several hours and then checked by a lab. The test determines if Radon Gas, known to be in that particular area of the country, has infiltrated the home and could pose a health threat.

3. **Lead-Based Paint:** Prevalent in the early 1970s and before, lead-based paint can be a health hazard if ingested. It is found in older painted surfaces, such as windowsills in homes. Paint scrapings are made of suspected areas and tested in a lab.

4. **Asbestos:** Found in older tile floors and ceilings, this substance has proven to be a health hazard and must be removed. In the case of ceilings, it can often be "encapsulated" by painting.

5. **Lots and Grounds:**
   - Walks, stoops, steps
   - Patios, balconies, porches, etc.
   - Retaining walls, such as seawalls (Seawalls may require an engineering survey.)
   - Drainage: Grading, swales, basement areas, window wells, etc.
   - Fences
   - Outside storage sheds

6. **Roof:**
   - General condition
   - Flashing

continued . . .

- Skylights
- Chimney
- Gutters and downspouts
- Signs of loose shingles or tiles
- Signs of leaking
- Signs of damaged shingles or tiles

7. **Exterior Surface of Home:**
   - Paint condition
   - Trim
   - Fascia
   - Soffitts

8. **Garage and Carports:**
   - Garage door
   - Automatic door opener
   - Structural condition

9. **Structure:**
   - Foundation condition
   - Beams
   - Load-bearing walls
   - Joists and trusses
   - Piers and posts
   - Floor or slab
   - Handrails

10. **Attic:**
    - Roof framing
    - Signs of leakage or water penetration
    - Sheathing
    - Ventilation
    - Attic fans (if any)

11. **Basement:**
    - Evidence of water penetration
    - Sump pump
    - Floor
    - Heated

continued . . .

12. **Crawl Space:**
    - Evidence of water penetration
    - Moisture
    - Access

13. **Electrical:**
    - Voltage- _____Amps- _____
    - Type of panel/circuit breakers
    - Ground
    - Service cable coming into home
    - Wiring up to code
    - Receptacles in working condition
    - Light switches in working condition

14. **Heating and Air Conditioning System:**
    - Primary operation
    - Draft control
    - Exhaust system
    - Fuel tanks and lines
    - Distribution system
    - Thermostat
    - Humidifier
    - Heat exchanger
    - Circulation fans, etc.
    - Condition and age of air conditioning system

15. **Plumbing:**
    - Water pipes
    - Drainpipes
    - Sewer lines
    - Laundry tubs
    - Water pressure

continued . . .

- Toilets
- Sinks and tubs
- Leaking faucets
- Clogged or partially clogged drains
- Water heater
  - Capacity
  - Age
  - Condition
  - Exhaust system where needed

16. Pool and/or Hot Tub:
- Pool type (above ground or in ground)
- Decking
- Heater
- Pump and filter system
- Fence
- Hot tub condition

17. Fireplace:
- Condition
- Flue
- Chimney

18. Kitchen:
- Range and oven
- Built-in microwave
- Dishwasher
- Disposal
- Ventilator
- Other built-ins

19. Well, Septic Tanks, etc. (if they apply)

continued . . .

Summary Page:

FINDINGS	ACTION REQUIRED	ESTIMATED COST

This is the final summary page that outlines any deficiencies found, what is needed to correct them and the estimated cost of the repairs.

CHAPTER 18

BANKS, MORTGAGE BROKERS, AND OTHER LENDERS

The first thing we need to do is identify the various sources of real estate financing (other than your rich uncle). Here is a brief description of the major types of lenders and how they operate.

BANKS AND SAVINGS AND LOAN ASSOCIATIONS

For decades, banks and S&Ls (savings and loan associations) were the primary, and often the only, sources of mortgage money for the average home buyer.

How they operate is simple to understand, as we have already pointed out. They have depositors who put money into savings accounts, CDs, etc., in their bank. They pay these depositors interest on those savings. They now loan out that money, subject to restrictions by the U.S. government, at a higher rate of interest than they must pay their depositors. Sounds simple. Almost all lenders use that same principle. Let's look at the other major players in the mortgage market.

MORTGAGE BROKERS

Mortgage brokers have an advantage over the local bank when you are seeking a mortgage. Your bank can quote financing based only on what is available from their depositors. Mortgage brokers deal with quite a few banks, S&Ls, and other lenders. They can give you a choice of where you place your mortgage based on the best terms, amount of loan, and ease of qualifying. There is a catch, however. They charge for their services. It may be a flat fee or a percentage (points) of the mortgage amount you borrow. You need to carefully compare what they have to offer with what you can do with a single lender.

Mortgage brokers have another advantage that you do not have. They also work with a large number of potential borrowers. This gives them a certain degree of clout. Lenders know that, if they treat the mortgage broker fairly, they stand to get a lot of business. Quite often, you can get a better loan or lower interest rate than if you applied for the loan yourself, even from the same lender. Once you get one or more quotes from a mortgage broker, factor in the charge for the service and select the best deal. By the way, you will probably get a choice of two or more lenders. Remember, we pointed out that lenders are in the business of loaning out money at a higher rate of interest than they have to pay their depositors. Mortgage interest rates, terms and availability of funds vary from lender to lender and from day to day. The mortgage broker is usually able to keep track of who has money to lend and at the best terms.

If you are having trouble obtaining a mortgage due to your credit rating or limited cash, some mortgage brokers may be able to help you more than a bank. For example, my wife, an active Realtor, has been able to get many marginal buyers into homes through a mortgage broker she uses regularly when the same conventional lenders turned the buyers down.

HOW MORTGAGE BANKERS DIFFER FROM MORTGAGE BROKERS

Unlike mortgage brokers, mortgage bankers generally get control of a sizable amount of money, sometimes millions of dollars. They contact banks, S&Ls and other types of lenders and, "lock in" these sizable funds at a fixed rate of interest and terms. They are gambling, in most cases, on interest rates increasing. If they are correct at guessing the market, they will be able to offer mortgage financing at a lower rate than current available rates from conventional lenders.

OTHER LENDERS

There are other lenders in the marketplace. Here are just a few:

PRIVATE LENDERS

You will often find ads in the newspaper from private individuals or groups that are willing to place mortgage loans. They may have money available at a lower interest rate than the going mortgage market. Some of them have funds in CDs, etc., that are paying 3% or 4% interest. An 8% mortgage, backed by a note from the borrower and secured by real estate, is an excellent investment for these individuals.

> **CAUTION:** You need to scrutinize these sources of funds. Be very careful of the terms and conditions of any loans placed through them. Quite often, you will incur stiff penalties if you are a day or two late with a payment. Watch out for short-term balloon mortgages or prepayment penalties. *It is best to seek legal advice before entering into this type of financing.* Don't get into a dangerous mortgage situation in order to save a couple of percent points on the interest rate.

INSURANCE COMPANIES

Although insurance companies have large sums of money to use for mortgage financing, they generally restrict their investments to large commercial properties and not single-family homes. But it never hurts to ask.

FHA AND VA FINANCING

FHA financing allows you to enter into a mortgage contract with a minimum amount of your own cash. Backed by the federal government, FHA loans, when available, can be especially helpful for a first-time home uyer.

If you are a veteran, you may qualify for a VA loan. Check with the government office for VA and get the details.

FRIENDS AND RELATIVES

Although not the best source of financing, don't overlook friends and relatives. Quite often a well-off relative may be willing to carry a mortgage for you. Keep in mind, however: Financial dealings with friends and relatives can often create a strain on the relationship. On the plus side, it could be an inexpensive place to obtain a home loan. If it's a choice of not getting your new home or trying to keep that rich uncle happy while in your new home, that uncle might not be so bad after all.

One Final Suggestion . . . This is the best suggestion of all. Try to talk the seller into carrying the mortgage, unless the cash out of the sale is needed for another home. Find out what the seller intends to do with the money, assuming the home is owned free and clear. If it is going to be put in a savings account, you can offer the seller a higher rate of interest than is available from the bank . . . and it will be secured by a mortgage and note. You also eliminate closing points and the strict qualifying process a commercial lender requires.

Whenever you need mortgage financing, don't hesitate to shop around for the best deal. Check with banks, mortgage brokers, the seller and even Uncle Harry. Always give yourself a choice. Don't settle on just one quote from one lender.

CHAPTER 19

REAL ESTATE
BROKERS

This chapter will give you a better understanding of how real estate brokers work and what they do for the professional fee they charge.

BROKER VS. REALTOR

Before we begin our discussion, we should review one point mentioned earlier in this book. What is the difference between a licensed real estate associate or broker and a Realtor?

Everyone who sells real estate must be licensed by the Department of Professional Regulation of the particular state. Realtors take their licensing one step further. They are members of the National Association of Realtors. As such they become members of the State Association of Realtors and their local area Board of Realtors. The national association has strict guidelines about how their Realtors must conduct business as well as a strong Code of Ethics under which they are expected to operate. While both Realtors and real estate associates and brokers are still subject to the laws and discipline of their State Department of Professional Regulation, Realtors are subject to additional discipline by the Realtor Association.

For simplicity throughout this book we have interchanged the terms Realtor, broker and real estate associate when we refer to anyone who is licensed by the state to sell real estate. It makes it easier to include everyone who is licensed to sell real estate.

The term "broker" generally refers to the owner of the real estate company who is licensed by the state to have an office and add associates.

I say, "add" associates because most real estate sales people are independent contractors; they are not employed. The broker handles funds on the sale of properties, furnishes desk space, and can even give assistance to the associates when they need it.

Real estate associates are generally considered to be those who are not licensed to operate their own office but who may work in a broker's office as sales persons.

Confused? Let's make it a little more confusing. The terms "broker" and "associate" are, in many states, used interchangeably when referring to "associates." Licensing law in those states will allow associates to call themselves real estate brokers, even though they are not licensed to operate their own office.

BROKER QUALIFICATIONS

If you decide to work with a real estate broker, because you just don't want the work involved in marketing your home yourself, you need to carefully select the right one. The first thing you should ask the broker or sales associate is "What are your qualifications?" Ask the following:

- *How active are you in this area?* (the one where your house is located, if you are a seller)

- *Are you part of the MLS system?* If you are a buyer, this gives you access to almost all the homes that are for sale in the area that is of interest to you. If you are a seller, your home will be exposed to all of the Realtors in the area or local board of Realtors. In fact, most Realtors boards have reciprocal agreements with the adjoining boards so your home listing may be available in the adjoining counties as well as your own.

- *What sales have you made in the area?*

- *How many listings do you or your office have in this area?*

- *Are you active full time in real estate?* Many brokers are part-timers. To know the market completely, the associate you select should be dedicated full time.

- *How do you market properties?* (if you are the seller)

- *How long have you been in real estate here?*

- *Do you have any professional degrees in real estate?* (such as CRB or Certified Residential Broker or GRI [Graduate of Realtor Institute]). These are symbols of continuing education.

You may not be comfortable in asking all of these questions, but the more you know about the qualifications of the broker you are about to employ, the better your decision will be.

Important Point: We specify asking if the broker is part of the MLS or Multiple Listing System. This listing service is generally a function of the Realtor Association. Unless the broker or sales associate and the office are Realtor members, they will not have access to the MLS system. I'm not saying that non-Realtors are not good sales associates; some are excellent. If, however, you feel that your property needs to be exposed to the entire real estate community, the MLS system is the best way to do it. Non-Realtors must depend on open houses, direct mailing, newspaper ads, etc., to give your listing exposure. Realtors not only use all of those marketing methods, but have the added advantage of belonging to the MLS system.

Having said that, I must now add that there is a possible exception to the rule of needing the MLS system to expose your property. If you live in a condominium complex or a private community (such as a country club), there may be a real estate broker or associate who owns a home there and devotes full time to marketing homes in that community. I know one such broker in that situation in a country club community. She "is" the broker in that area. Even though other real estate brokers live in the same community, she is the one who makes herself known to every resident through continual mailings and active participation. As a result, she lists and sells the majority of homes there. She happens to be a

Realtor, but would do just as well without the Realtor association as long as she sticks only with that community.

Many sellers will contact her, only because of her track record for selling homes in the area, plus the fact that she makes certain everyone living there knows who she is. Perhaps you have such a broker in your community or neighborhood. Drive around and see who has the most "for sale" signs in front of houses. Watch for mailings from different brokers. If they are good, they will probably send you continual mailings stating, "I just listed . . ." or "I just sold." You can see that they are active in the market.

HOW BROKERS OPERATE

Every real estate office, whether Realtor or real estate broker offices, operate differently. Here are some facts you should know.

HOW BROKERS GET LISTINGS

In order to get a listing, many brokers resort to one or two tactics.

Tactic Number One:

"I have a buyer looking for a home just like yours." (And if you believe that, I have some swampland for sale in the Florida Everglades.) This response will often come as soon as you put your FSBO sign in the front yard. In most cases, they are looking for listings. Since you are marketing the home yourself, you can say, "Just bring your prospect around. If that person wants to buy my home, I'll be happy to pay you a commission." Chances are you won't hear from that broker again.

Tactic Number Two:

Some brokers will offer to list your home at a price that far exceeds your expectations. If you have a home listed at $150,000 and you did your homework, you know that you have it priced at fair market value. All of a sudden a broker tells you that you can get $200,000 if you list with that office. Don't believe it! We discussed this earlier in the book.

ADVERTISING

Most real estate brokers advertise listings. Here are some common ways most properties are exposed to the buying public.

1. *Sign on the Property:* This is usually the first step a broker takes and it is the form of advertising that will probably draw the biggest response . . . at least for the first week or two. Many potential buyers drive through neighborhoods and copy down phone numbers from signs on properties that are of interest to them.

2. *Newspaper Advertising:* One thing you need to know about newspaper ads was mentioned in the seller section of this book. Brokers run ads in newspapers for two primary reasons. The first is to keep the seller happy. (A seller wants to see the property advertised.) The second reason is to pick up potential home buyers.

   Now comes the fact that most home sellers never know. When a broker runs an ad on your home, chances are remote that the caller will buy your home. The ad is run to get buyers to call. If they happen to be interested in the home that was advertised, that is a bonus. The broker's goal, however, is to locate buyers for a home and not necessarily yours. On the plus side, it all evens out. Potential buyers may call on another home and end up liking yours better. This is one good reason to list your home with someone who can show the majority of homes in an area . . . the MLS system. If your broker does not have a buyer for your home, there is a good chance another MLS member will.

3. *Magazine Advertising:* There are publications in most cities that specialize in listing homes for sale. Your broker may place an ad for your home in one of these publications. They have a large circulation among people who may not see a newspaper ad.

4. *Open Houses:* Expect your broker to hold one or more open houses. They will be scheduled usually on weekends when home buyers are free to look. Keep in mind, however, that most visitors will not be interested in your home. The broker wants to sell his or her own listing, but if a couple of sincere buyers for any home can be picked up along the way, so much the better.

5. *Broker Open House:* The listing agent for your home will probably want to hold a broker open house and invite all of the local brokers to see the home.

6. *Brochures:* Although MLS members will have copies of the MLS listing to hand out and mail to prospects, a good broker will also prepare an advertising brochure or mailer, with photo(s) to expose your home to as many people as possible.

7. *The Internet:* You may list with a broker who actively advertises listings on the Internet. It is the marketing medium of the future that is available today. Unfortunately, most brokers do not know how to do it properly. They may put it on their site, but will get few if any visitors.

Point of Interest: Do not expect your broker to continually advertise your home in many different ways. As a practical matter, two things enter into the decision to advertise.

First, the selling price of the home. Remember, the broker gets paid nothing until the home is sold. In the meantime, all advertising and promotional expenses are out-of-pocket. If you are selling a $100,000 home and the listing broker expects to get a 3% commission, assuming a broker in another office sells the property, that is $3,000. Out of that $3,000, the listing sales associate gets a share, maybe as much as sixty to eighty percent. If the listing associate gets sixty percent, the office is left with forty percent of $3,000 or $1,200. The broker who expects to maintain a real estate office, with all of the expenses involved, cannot spend too much of that $1,200 on advertising. If the home, for whatever reason, does not sell, then the office is out all of the advertising costs.

Second, the broker who has an active business, with quite a few associates and many listings, cannot afford to keep all of them in the paper at all times. The ads will generally be rotated so that each homeowner is represented at least part of the time. Keep in mind what we mentioned earlier: The main purposes of an ad are to get the phone to ring and to pick up a potential buyer.

Floor Time and Leads

Most real estate offices have floor time for their associates. It may be called "lead" or "opportunity time" or any number of names. Basically, each associate takes a turn "on floor" and any phone calls or walk-ins belong to the floor person. Each office has exceptions to this rule. Sign calls or ad calls may go the listing agent, no matter who takes the call.

Important Point: A prospect to buy or sell a home belongs to no one. Walk-ins, unless a specific broker in the office is requested, go to the floor person, except as noted above. There is a common rule that all brokers are supposed to abide by. It is "procuring cause of sale." This means that, in loose terms, whoever gets the signed contract is the procuring cause of sale and entitled to the commission. This does not give one associate the right to deliberately pirate the prospect from an associate who is working with that person. Occasionally a prospect just does not like a particular associate and will seek out someone else. There is nothing wrong with that.

"Farms" and Territories

Another factor that often affects who gets what prospect is the office policy for associates who specialize in an area. Most real estate offices encourage each associate to select an area of the city that is of most interest. It may be, and is probably best, that the listing area is in the neighborhood in which the associate lives. Real estate brokers generally refer to these areas as "farms." The associate should "farm" or be in continual contact with everyone in the "farm" area through periodic mailings and personal contacts. I mentioned earlier the woman in the country club community. She rarely lets a week go by without filling in all of the area residents on what she has listed or sold or news of the community. That's why they all know her . . . and call her when they want to sell.

Getting back to the subject at hand. If an office has associates "working" a territory, any prospects that are generated for that area may be directed to that associate. Chances are good they came into the office as a result of that associate's sign that they saw in that neighborhood.

Important Point: Although a real estate office may have listing farms or territories, and you want to have a home in a sales associate's territory, you are not obligated to list your home with that associate. If you have a friend in that same office, you can always request that person to be your listing agent. Your broker friend, depending on office policy, may have to pay the farm area associate a referral fee when the home is sold.

Why would anyone do this? It's an accepted fact that one of the best ways a broker can obtain listings and become known is to concentrate all efforts in a certain area. As added incentive to do so, the office tries to insure that any leads that come in from that broker's territory go to that broker.

Earlier, I suggested using a Realtor to obtain a free CMA, even though you intend to sell the home yourself. If you end up doing this, call back that broker and say that you will provide a list of names and phone numbers of people who registered with you when they looked at your home. You are giving the broker something in return for the favor done for you.

THE BROKER'S COMMISSION

There are some things you need to know about the broker's real estate professional fee (commission). First of all, it is not a rate established by the National Association of Realtors, the local real estate boards, or the state real estate Department of Professional Regulation.

Each individual real estate office or company establishes its own real estate professional fees. That's the law! You should *never* hear a real estate broker tell you, "I can't cut my commission because it is set by the Board of Realtors." What you should hear is, "I cannot cut my commission because it is set by our office policy."

It also needs to be understood that office policy is not based on what other area real estate companies are charging. Again, it's against federal law to say or do this.

Now for the meat of this discussion. Real estate brokers don't want you to know this, but their fee is not set in stone, even if their office specifies a set fee for all services. It is not uncommon for a broker to agree to a commission less than the rate established by its office. How much is that set rate? It will vary anywhere from 3% or 4% up to 7% or 8% of the sale price. Quite often, vacant land and businesses (where no real estate is included) will be listed with upwards to a 10% fee.

Here is another point of interest. Generally, the larger the property value, the lower the overall commission rate will be. A property up to a million dollars may be listed with a 6% professional fee. A five-million-dollar property, however, may bear a 6% fee on the first million dollars, a 5% fee on the next million, and a 4% fee on the balance. Fee structure can vary from property to property and/or real estate office to real estate office. In support of the real estate broker, most of them earn their fees. They perform all of the services that you are learning about in this book, plus many more. Once you read the section on real estate brokers, I think you will have a different outlook.

Remember, they do not get paid until a sale and closing takes place. They spend a lot of time and money getting to that point. I'd hate to tell you the countless hours I have invested in buyers or sellers, to the point of contract negotiation, only to have the deal fall apart through no fault of my own. Unlike attorneys, we have to finalize a transaction and have a closing before we collect that first dollar.

Speaking of attorneys, let me digress a little and tell you about one particularly obnoxious attorney I had the "privilege" of working with on the closing of a million-dollar office building sale I had made. The work was done, the contract signed by all parties, and the amount of the real estate professional fee agreed to be paid by the seller was written in the contract.

The closing was going smoothly, everything signed, when the attorney looked at me and asked, "Now, what are we going to do about your real estate commission?" Needless to say, my mouth dropped open in dismay.

"What do you mean?" I finally asked.

"How much are you willing to cut your commission? After all, you guys get paid an awful lot for the little bit of work you do." The eyes of all the buyers, sellers and other attorneys in the room were all riveted on me.

My response was, "When I can justify charging my clients $265.00 an hour, just for the privilege of talking to me, like you do, I'll be able to reduce my fees."

My first thought was, "I just blew that deal." To my surprise, the conversation was immediately dropped, the transaction closed . . . and I got paid . . . the full amount that was due.

There are other concessions you can possibly obtain from a broker in order to make the transaction more attractive. Perhaps you need additional cash beyond what you have available. The broker may be willing to take part of the commission in the form of a second mortgage in order to reduce the cash needed at closing.

Although it will not be well received by the broker, a deferred commission is also possible. Perhaps the seller needs all the cash for a new home purchase, but will be able to pay the broker in six months when additional funds become available. Expect the broker to require a personal note executed by the seller, guaranteeing payment within a certain period of time, and will probably want the note to be interest bearing.

Commission Splits

Let's go back to our $150,000 home and assume it was listed with a 6% professional fee. Keep in mind that each office sets its own real estate professional fees and establishes how they are to be divided within the office. If the home sells at the full $150,000, the total fee will be $9,000. If another office sells the listing, that fee may be split on a 50/50 basis which leaves the listing office with $4,500. Depending on the fee split in that office, the associate may get fifty to ninety percent of that fee. (Ninety percent or higher if the associate is paying all or most of the expenses plus rent for the desk space in the office.) If the real estate office receives forty percent of that $4,500, it will receive $1,800 when the home sells and closes.

There is also a situation where the sales associate will have to pay a cooperating broker a referral fee out of his or her portion of the commission. Why? We already mentioned the listing farm situation. Another example is where an associate is too busy to handle a prospect so that prospect is referred to a fellow associate and thereafter collects a referral fee if that prospect buys a home or lists a home that sells.

As you can see, those "big" fees can be split up into some pretty small pieces. What is even worse, sometimes the transaction will never close and the broker ends up with nothing except a lot of wasted time and expense . . . but that's the real estate business.

DISCOUNT BROKERS AND FEE DISCOUNTING

Discount brokers have become quite popular in some areas. They will accept a listing on your home and agree to a commission much lower than most of the offices in town. You can expect to receive a lot fewer services from discount brokers. Someone once made the comment that "You get what you pay for." If you go with a discount broker, just to save money, stop to consider this:

How much will that broker do to promote your home for the small fee you are paying? Chances are good that such a broker does not belong to the MLS system, so exposure will be reduced. We have already mentioned the small commission that is left after fee splits. From that, advertising must be paid, an office leased and maintained, and office expenses covered. If someone is willing to list your home and charge you only $250 to do it, you have a pretty good idea of how much money can be spent promoting it. These brokers usually rely on a large volume of listings with minimum expenses on each to be successful and profitable.

REPRESENTATION AND ETHICS

When you employ a broker to sell your home or to buy a home, you expect to be treated fairly. Realtors must abide by their strict code of ethics, but non-Realtors are also expected to do the same in order to comply with the State Department of Professional Regulation. Most states can assess severe penalties on associates and broker offices that breach their ethical conduct. These penalties can include fines, suspension or revocation of their license or even jail sentences for severe breaches of conduct. The law, in most states, carries it one step further. A broker who is found guilty of a major crime, not associated with real estate, is still subject to the possible revocation of the real estate license.

This brings us to the "sticky" point of the real estate law. What can and should a broker tell a buyer or seller? Let's assume the seller of a property tells the broker: "I'm asking $150,000 but I'll probably take $125,000." Unless the seller specifically agrees to let the broker tell a buyer that, and does it in writing, the broker cannot suggest it to a buyer. If a potential buyer says, "I like the home but I think it is overpriced. What do you think the seller will take?" All the broker can tell the buyer is, "Why don't you make an offer and we'll submit it to the seller?"

Conversely, you know that a buyer is really motivated to buy a home. The couple has already closed on the sale of its home and the furniture is in a moving van in a parking lot. The broker cannot suggest to a seller that the buyer is desperate to buy and will probably pay any asking price as long as the closing is in one week.

KEEPING IN TOUCH

Your broker should stay in contact with you continually and should keep you updated on any activity. You should see copies of ads and brochures being run and hear about the results of a showing to a potential buyer. You should be contacted even if there is not any positive or important news, just to let you know there is still active work going on in regard to your home listing.

CHAPTER 20

TITLE COMPANIES AND ATTORNEYS

You may do all of the listing or selling of your home yourself, or locate and buy a home on your own, but you will still have to work with a title company or attorney to handle the closing on the sale.

TITLE COMPANIES

Title companies are the people who furnish you with a title policy on your home. This protects you from any unforeseen ownership problems now or in the future. It's like a life insurance policy. And, like that, you hope you will never have to use it.

A title insurance policy not only insures you while you own the home, but also after you sell. For example, you sell your home and twenty years later, the third buyer after you owned it discovers there was a problem with the title during the time you owned the home. Again, your title company will resolve it. Now you know why buying title insurance is a must for home buyers.

Most land titles can be traced back to the days when the property was purchased (or stolen) from the Native Americans. A lot can happen in that length of time. People who are long since gone can have great-great grandchildren who suddenly discover they have a claim on that property.

Title companies generally employ attorneys to handle all of the legal implications of selling property and examining the chain of title on a property. You can often have the title company handle the closing for you.

A Word of Caution: If you have the title company representatives handle the closing, keep in mind that they are probably really representing themselves and not you. Their primary fiduciary relationship is with the title company that employs them, so you may not get complete representation. On the other hand, if you are a seller and know, from looking at a closing statement, how much money you should get at closing, you may feel you do not need an attorney or a title company. As long as you have a check for your proceeds, that is all you need.

Buyers, on the other hand, have to be certain they are getting clear title to the property and things are all in order. Again, the title company will not write a title policy unless it is reasonably sure there are no problems. Buyers also need to be certain the deed is recorded promptly after the closing, showing them as the new titleholders.

Title company fees are generally based on the selling price of the property; the company will furnish you with a schedule of fees. They could range anywhere from a few hundred dollars to several thousand, depending on the property price. The good news is that it is a one-time fee that is good forever.

SIMULTANEOUS ISSUE OF TITLE POLICIES

If you are placing a new mortgage on the property you are buying, or buying it subject to an existing mortgage, the lender will also require a title insurance policy to cover its interest (the mortgage amount) in the property. If you buy a $150,000 home, and have a $100,000 mortgage, you will need a $150,000 policy and the lender will also have a policy in the amount of $100,000. You must pay for both. It is possible, and you should find out how, to have both policies written simultaneously. That way only one title search will have to be done. Whoever writes the two policies should give you a sizable discount. I've seen cases where a buyer pays full price for the larger title policy and only $50 to $100 for the second one—a big savings. It's worth checking into with the closing agent(s). The only catch is that the same attorney will have to write both policies, so you may be locked in on the closing agent chosen by the lender.

WHO PAYS FOR A TITLE POLICY?

Until now, we have indicated that it's the buyer who pays for the title policy. But all costs in a real estate transaction are negotiable, including this one. Although the buyer usually pays for it (the one who wants the protection), there are no rules saying the seller cannot agree to pay all or part of the cost.

The seller is obligated to give clear title to the property. In many areas of the country, the only way the seller can guarantee clear title is with a title insurance policy. In that case, it is customary for the seller to furnish it and pay for it.

Everything is negotiable in a purchase and sale contract. It does not hurt to try.

ATTORNEYS

You may also want to use your attorney as the closing agent on the purchase or sale of your property. Just be certain you use an attorney who specializes in or has a lot of experience in real estate closings. In today's world, there are specialists in every phase of law. You do not need a high-priced, high-profile criminal attorney to close on your home, one who may be totally inexperienced in that area of law.

You may also find that your attorney will insist on preparing the offer-to-purchase contract you use when buying a home. If you feel very unsure of a generic contract or in your ability to prepare a legal contract that protects you, an attorney may be the answer. In some states, real estate brokers are not even allowed to write a purchase contract, even the pre-printed one that has been authored by the Board of Realtors and its attorneys in that state.

You need to watch your costs carefully. I've worked with some attorneys who did an excellent job with their clients. I've also worked with others who insisted on preparing and using a ten-page, legal-size document. Not only did it cost the client a bundle of money, but often frightened away the seller. Any seller who did want to review it had to take it to another attorney to translate all of its legalese.

DECIDING TO USE A REAL ESTATE BROKER

Chances are you will be successful selling or buying a home on your own, if you follow the tips in this book. The information you have learned is based on what successful real estate brokers have known and used to become million-dollar sales people. You have learned not only how to successfully sell or buy a home yourself, but you have been exposed to the mistakes home sellers and buyers often make and how to avoid them. However, there may be circumstances under which you would want to use a real estate broker.

SELLING WITH A BROKER

Before you decide to use a broker, check six selling factors:

1. Is your home priced at fair market value?

2. Are other comparable homes in your area selling but yours is not?

3. Does your home show well?

4. Have you made a continual effort to promote and market your home?

5. Are you in a slow market where nothing much is selling?

6. Are you sick and tired of the work and time involved in marketing your home, and you'd rather pay a broker a fee to do the work for you?

If you answer "yes" to all of the above, you may want to consider listing your home with a broker. If you do, don't expect miracles. You agreed that you have followed the above six rules for selling a home and have been unsuccessful. There is a good chance a broker will also have problems as well. You need to explain to the broker what you have done and let the broker suggest how to do things differently to get the results you desire. A Realtor, for example, has access to the Multiple Listing System, so your home will be exposed to every Realtor in the marketing area, many of whom may have potential buyers for your home. Use the Broker Listing Questionnaire on page 217 in selecting your broker.

A *final word:* Unless you are in a buyer's market, where homes are not selling, there is no reason you will not be successful in selling your home yourself if you followed the suggestions in this book.

BUYING WITH A BROKER

As a buyer, you may have become discouraged trying to locate the right home for you at the price you can afford. Before calling a broker, answer these questions:

1. Did you continually check the "For Sale By Owner" ads in the newspaper?

2. Did you drive in the areas that are of interest and look for FSBO signs?

3. Did you try searching for a home on the Internet?

4. Did you research the home market enough to know you are shopping in the right area for your budget, and did you get pre-qualified for a mortgage?

5. Are you being flexible with your demands? You may have to accept a lesser home for a couple of years until your financial situation or the market changes.

If you answer "yes" to all of the above, you may want to consider using a broker to help you buy a home. Realtors have access to listings, through the Multiple Listing System, that you would not be able to locate yourself. As you were driving through the various neighborhoods that were of interest to you, you may have seen several broker signs on properties that may be of interest to you.

A particular broker who has several signs in the neighborhood may be a good one to call. That broker is probably "farming" that area. Be sure to use the Broker Listing Questionnaire on page 217 to help you select your broker.

*A **final word:*** Unless you are in a seller's market, where there are very few homes available for sale, you will have no problems finding the right home for you at a price you can afford to pay if you followed the suggestions in this book.

Broker Listing Questionnaire

Here is a list of questions you would like answered by a broker whom you are considering to list your home. Don't expect to get answers to all of these questions. Many brokers probably have never been asked some of them before.

Broker Track Record:

____ Listings

____ Sales

____ Marketing Area

____ Do you concentrate on this area (in which your home is located)?

____ Special education (GRI [Graduate of Realtor Institute], etc.)

Broker Services and Listing Agreement:

____ Did broker furnish you with a resume, track record, details about company?

____ Did broker furnish you with a CMA?

____ How do you determine the fair market value of my home?

____ How do you advertise a listing?

    ____ Newspaper, magazines *(Tiger Tale)*

    ____ Brochures

    ____ Mailings to other brokers, prospects, neighbors, etc.

    ____ Internet

    ____ Other _____

____ Are you an MLS member?

____ What is your office commission rate?

____ How long a listing do you need?

____ Disclosure statement (Whom do you represent)

____ Did broker give you a listing presentation?

Current Market Condition:

____ How is the seller market now?

____ What is selling and at what price?

Marketing Your Home:

____ Office tour

____ Broker open house

____ Regularly scheduled open houses for the public

____ Do you pre-qualify prospects for my home before showing it?

____ How do you keep me informed of what is happening—(follow-up & feedback)?

____ Show my home only by appointment?

____ Do you accompany another broker who shows my home (not really necessary)?

____ Does broker make suggestions on how to make my home more salable (what needs to be done)?

GLOSSARY

Here are the most common terms you will hear when discussing residential real estate.

ACCELERATION CLAUSE: The lender has the right to require the entire remaining balance of a mortgage as due and payable if ever the borrower misses a certain number of payments. (Note: That is why you need to sit down with a lender if you are having trouble meeting payments, before the debt reaches the point of being "called." You can often work out a payment schedule you both can live with.)

ADJUSTABLE RATE MORTGAGE (ARM): The interest rate on this type of loan can vary depending on current mortgage rates, the cost of living, or other factors spelled out by a lender. There is generally a "cap" put on an ARM. For example, interest rates cannot be increased more than 2% in any one year or 6% total over the term of the mortgage. (Note: Accept this type of mortgage if no better terms are available. If you do accept an ARM, be sure you have reasonable annual and total rate caps on the loan.)

ADJUSTED COST BASIS: This is the value of your home, according to the IRS, at the time you sell. It is the selling price minus what you paid for the property, minus any capital improvements you have made, and minus your cost of sale. This topic is covered in detail in the book.

ALL-INCLUSIVE DEED OF TRUST: Also called a "wraparound mortgage." The mortgage "wraps" an existing mortgage. See complete details in the Mortgage section of this book.

ANNUAL PERCENTAGE RATE (APR): The interest rate charged by the lender.

AS IS: If a home is being sold "as is," the buyer has agreed to accept the home in whatever condition it presently is in. The seller will make no repairs and does not warrant the condition. It is up to the buyer and the home inspector to determine if it makes sense to purchase the home in an "as is" condition.

APPRAISAL: An estimate of market value of a home, prepared by a licensed property appraiser.

APPRECIATION: The amount your home increases in value while you own it. This is due to increase in the overall market and economy plus any capital improvements you may have made.

ASSESSED VALUE: The value the tax assessor establishes for a home. It is generally less than its market value.

ASSUMABLE MORTGAGE: A mortgage that can be assumed by a buyer. This must be carefully checked by a buyer to insure that the same terms and conditions hold true as for the present owner. Lenders may have the right to increase interest, reduce the term, etc.

BALLOON MORTGAGE: The loan may be amortized over a thirty-year period but the remaining balance (balloon amount) may be due and payable at the end of the tenth year. We discuss this subject in the Mortgage Loan section of the book.

BRIDGE LOAN: A temporary loan that allows the seller of a home to obtain necessary funds to close on a new home. This is ideal if home sellers must close on a new home before the funds are received from the home they are selling.

BROKER: Someone licensed by the state to sell, list, rent and appraise real estate. In the Broker section of the book we discuss the difference between real estate brokers and Realtors.

BUYER'S BROKER: The buyer employs the broker to locate a home and pays the broker the agreed-upon real estate professional fee. The broker represents the buyer.

CAPITAL GAIN: The portion of the profits from the sale of a home that may be subject to tax.

CLOSING COSTS: The funds needed, above and beyond the purchase price of the home, to close on the transaction. These include such items as tax and insurance prorations, mortgage closing costs, title insurance, etc.

COACH HOUSE HOMES: Coach house homes are not too prevalent in most areas. They are basically three-story homes. The ground floor is usually the garage and laundry and storage area, the second floor is the living area and the third floor has bedrooms.

COMMISSIONS: The fee real estate brokers charge for listing and selling a home. Most brokers refer to the commission as a "real estate professional fee."

COMMON AREA: The area, generally associated with condominiums, which is for use by all tenants and not owned by any of them. This includes common hallways, the recreation area and clubhouse, parking lot, etc.

COMPARATIVE MARKET ANALYSIS (CMA): The process of determining the value of a home by what has sold in the immediate area that is comparable to the subject property.

CONDOMINIUMS AND COOPERATIVES: Condominium apartments are in a large complex in which unit owners have title to their own apartment and share the common areas. Cooperative apartment owners do not have title to their units but rather shares in the stock that owns the entire complex. Both have monthly assessments to cover the cost of maintaining the common areas and support staff salaries.

COUNTER OFFERS: Once a contract is submitted to a seller, the seller will usually want to make some changes in the contract. The price or terms may not be acceptable as offered. The seller will make a counter offer, changing items, and initialing the changes. The buyer then has the option to accept the changes or make a "counter-counter offer." See the complete discussion in the Offer-to-Purchase Contract section of this book.

DEBT-TO-INCOME RATIO: The formula used by lenders to determine how large a monthly mortgage payment you can afford to pay based on your income and other monthly debts.

DEED: The document giving you title to the property. It is recorded at the courthouse in the county in which the property is located.

DEFAULT: If you fall behind in mortgage payments, you are in default. This, according to the terms written in the mortgage, gives the lender an option to take necessary steps to protect its interest in the property. See also Acceleration Clause.

DISCLOSURE STATEMENT: This can contain several disclosures: The lender gives you a disclosure statement that spells out the exact terms of the loan. (You agree to a 9% mortgage, but the actual annual percentage rate will be higher. This will be spelled out in the disclosure statement.) The seller may give you a disclosure statement stating that, to the best of his or her knowledge, there are no defects in the home other than those already noted. Real estate brokers will give you a disclosure statement outlining which party, if either, to the transaction they represent.

DOWN PAYMENT: The amount of cash you give with an offer-to-purchase contract. It's a "good faith" deposit, held in escrow, until the property closes or the contract is declared null and void and the deposit refunded to the buyer. See the chapter on Contracts for more complete details.

EQUITY: The amount of "cash value" you have in a property. (What the property sells for minus the mortgage amount.)

ESCROW: A trust account, established by a neutral third party such as a real estate broker, attorney or title company. The deposit that accompanies a contract is held in this account.

EXCLUSIVE AGENCY LISTING: The seller gives one broker the exclusive right to offer a property for sale, but reserves the right to sell it personally without being obligated to pay a real estate professional fee. This is a formal written document.

EXCLUSIVE RIGHT TO SELL: This is the normal listing contract between the seller and a broker. It gives the listing broker the exclusive right to sell the property, cooperate with other brokers and even be entitled to a fee if the seller sells it personally.

FAIR MARKET VALUE: The price, usually determined by a CMA, at which the property should sell, based on the sale of comparable properties in the area.

FIXED-RATE MORTGAGE: The interest rate and term will not vary during the life of the loan. Monthly payments, therefore, will also remain fixed or the same each month. (Note: The only possible variation of the monthly payments will be increases in taxes and insurance, if they are included as "escrow" payments with the mortgage payment.)

FLOOD INSURANCE: Some areas are considered to have a very high possibility of flooding. In these situations, the lender may require a flood insurance policy to insure against that eventuality.

FORECLOSURE: The act of a lender taking ownership of a property due to default on mortgage payments. Be sure to read the section of the book that explains what you need to do if you are in financial trouble.

FSBO: The acronym for "For Sale By Owner." Pronounced "fizzbo," it is the term given to homeowners who sell their home themselves.

GRADUATED-PAYMENT MORTGAGE: The mortgage is set up with lower payments during the earlier years which gradually increase over the term of the loan. This gives new home buyers, with limited income, the chance to own a home and increase the monthly payments as their ability to pay more increases.

HOME EQUITY LOAN: Some lenders, often private lenders, will make loans based on the equity you have in your home. (Your equity is the market value of the home minus current mortgage balance.)

HOME INSPECTIONS: An inspection of a home being sold. This is generally a complete inspection of the entire home, including the items shown under Home Warranty Plans. The buyer should always have an inspection made to insure that there are no major problems that are not easily visible.

HOMEOWNER INSURANCE: If you have a mortgage on your property, the lender will require you to carry a homeowner insurance policy. As a practical matter, you need the protection of your property. This policy protects you against loss from fire, wind, rain and other natural disasters. It should also be written to cover your possessions within the home. In order to keep costs down, you can get a higher deductible coverage.

HOME WARRANTY PLANS: Companies that cover the major areas of your home subject to breakdown, repair or replacement. These include appliances, heating/air conditioning systems, plumbing, electrical, roof and termite damage.

LEASE-OPTION: A potential home buyer enters into a lease-option with the seller of the property by agreeing to lease the home, at a given rental rate, until enough equity is available to purchase it. This is ideal, assuming the seller can afford to do it, for someone who does not have the equity to purchase now. The seller will generally allow a certain portion of the monthly payment to apply toward an eventual down payment. The option portion of the agreement gives the potential buyer the "option" to eventually close on the purchase or to simply walk away and decide not to buy. You can see the potential problems for a seller.

LIEN: The encumbrance or legal claim against a property. It is a formal document, generally filed with the courthouse, against the property. If the property is sold, that lien must be satisfied (paid off).

LISTING BROKER: The real estate broker who has a listing or exclusive right to sell the property.

LISTING CONTRACT: The legal contract between the seller and the real estate broker, giving the broker the legal right to offer the property for sale or lease at a specified price and terms.

MORTGAGE BROKER: An individual or company licensed by the state to place mortgages with borrowers. See the complete information in the Mortgage chapter of this book.

MORTGAGE INSURANCE: A policy on the property that the lender requires. It protects the lender in the event of the death of the borrower. You can usually have the requirement for this policy to be waived once you have sufficient equity in the property.

PARTNERSHIPS: Two or more people enter into a contract to jointly own property. An attorney should prepare the formal documents.

POINTS: The fee charged by the lender to create a mortgage for a borrower. It is actually a percentage of the mortgage amount. (Two points would be two percent of the mortgage amount.)

PREPAYMENT PENALTY: Some lenders may require that a penalty be paid if the mortgage is paid off prior to its normal expiration. The lender wants to know that loans that are placed will continue to draw interest for a given period of years.

PRINCIPAL PAYMENT: That portion of the mortgage payment that pays down the remaining balance on a mortgage. As you no doubt know, the principal portion of a mortgage is a very small part of the payment during the early years and increases as the loan balance is paid down.

PROPERTY TAX: The state, county and city tax on a property.

PRORATIONS: The payment of a portion of certain items at closing. For example, a buyer who is assuming the property insurance will owe the seller whatever portion of the policy has already been paid from the day of closing on. If the seller has paid for a home warranty program a year in advance, and the buyer intends to assume that coverage, the buyer will credit the seller for the unused portion of that policy.

REALTOR: A designation given to real estate brokers who belong to a local, state and the National Association of Realtors. They subscribe to a strict code of ethics. Realtors also have access to countless continuing education courses that further their knowledge and professionalism. They are also the group that established the MLS system to share listings with other members.

RIGHT OF RESCISSION: This clause gives the buyer the right to get out of the contract within three days after it has been executed by all parties. Occasionally the buyer may have a change of heart or have a panic attack and want out of the contract.

TITLE INSURANCE: A one-time insurance policy buyers MUST have for protection from any title or ownership problems during the period of property ownership and against any problems that may arise after they sell but which occurred while they owned it.

TOWN HOMES: Two-story homes, usually with the living quarters on the first floor and bedrooms on the second.

WRAPAROUND MORTGAGE: Also known as an "all inclusive deed of trust." This mortgage wraps around an existing mortgage. See the chapter on Mortgages in this book.

ZONING: Rules and written regulations by a city, county and state that allow and disallow certain uses for land. They also include such things as setback requirements, density and land use.

ABOUT THE AUTHOR

Milt Tanzer has been a real estate broker and Realtor since 1967. He owned his own large residential real estate office for several years. While active in the office ownership, he was a member and chairman of the local Board of Realtors Professional Standards Committee and a member of the Education Committee. He held the professional designation of Certified Commercial Investment Member (CCIM) of the National Association of Realtors while he was actively engaged in commercial/ investment real estate brokerage.

How to Buy or Sell Your Home Without a Broker is the fourth book Milt Tanzer has written for Prentice Hall. His first book, *Real Estate Investments and How to Make Them,* was published in 1975. Since then it has sold over a quarter of a million copies and is currently in its third edition.

Milt lives with his wife and oldest daughter in Deerfield Beach, Florida. His e-mail address is: mtanzer@att.net.

He has four Web sites devoted to real estate:

http://www.home-buyer-seller-tips.com is filled with free ideas and tips for home buyers and sellers, and is based on this book.

http://www.home-buyer-seller-tips.com/bkrfsbo.htm offers an online course for real estate brokers and contains an unbelievable program for finding and listing For Sale By Owner homes.

http://www.realestate-supermarket.com offering some outstanding software programs and digital forms, etc., for home buyers, sellers and brokers.

He also has a Web site for investors, *http://www.investmentre.com,* which has been considered by many investors as the "bible" for real estate investing. It is filled with free tips and ideas for beginners as well as seasoned pros.

INDEX

A

Abstracts of title, 70

Adjusted cost basis, and profit computation, 75-76

Advertising. *See* Marketing home

Age
  condo bylaw, 96
  tax exclusion on profit, 74

Air conditioning, pre-sale repairs, 58

All Inclusive Deeds of Trust, 171

Amortization
  short-term versus long-term, 165-66
  See also Mortgage options

Appliances
  "attached" items, 48
  inspection, 58

Appraisal of home
  appraised value versus fair market value, 66
  comparative market analysis (CMA), 15-17, 182-84
  and fair market value, 14-15
  importance of, 182-83
  income approach to value method, 185
  replacement cost method, 184-85

Appraisers
  lender as, 66, 183
  real estate broker as, 181-82

Appreciation of home
  factors related to, 90

and lease/option arrangement, 115

Asbestos, removal of, 60

Assessments, maintained community, 98-99

Assumed mortgage
  contract clause, 145
  nonassumable mortgages, 177
  and seller's escrow account, 159

Atmosphere, during showings, 20, 21, 32

Attorneys
  as closing agent, 213
  fees as closing cost, 70

B

Backup contract, 45

Balloon mortgages, 170, 176

Banks
  as appraiser, 66, 183
  escrow account, 37, 38, 126-28
  as financing source, 195
  and mortgage brokers, 196
  mortgage fees, 154-56

Bill of sale, personal property, 38

Board of directors, condominium, 96

Board of Realtors, 199, 206

Bridge loans, 43, 72-73, 84

Brochures
  broker preparation of, 204
  for marketing home, 24

D